Contemporary Perspectives on Developing Societies

Series Editors
JOHN MUKUM MBAKU
Weber State University, Ogden, Utah, USA
MWANGI S. KIMENYI
The University of Connecticut, USA

porary Perspectives on Developing Societies series was founded to serve
or policy relevant research. Books published in this series provide rigorous
issues relevant to the peoples of the Third World and their efforts to
ir participation in the global economy.

series

ed.) (2004), *Agenda Setting and Public Policy in Africa*.
.S., Mbaku, J.M. and Mwaniki, N. (eds) (2003), *Restarting and Sustaining
ic Growth and Development in Africa: The Case of Kenya*.
B.K. and Rwomire, A. (eds) (2003), *Human Impact on Environment and
ble Development in Africa*.
R.G (ed.) (2002), *Religion and Politics in the Developing World: Explosive
ions*.
2002), *The Challenges of Economic and Institutional Reforms in Africa*.
I., Agbese, P.O. and Kimenyi, M.S. (eds) (2001), *Ethnicity and Governance
hird World*.
(2001), *Southern Cameroons, 1922-1961: A Constitutional History*.
(ed.) (2001), *The Issue of Political Ethnicity in Africa*.
, P.J. (2000), *Justice in Africa: Rwanda's Genocide, its Courts, and the UN
l Tribunal*.
1. (ed.) (1999), *Preparing Africa for the Twenty-First Century*.
a, P.J. (ed.) (1999), *Middle East and North Africa: Governance,
atization, Human Rights*.
1.S., Wieland, R.C. and Von Pischke, J.D. (eds) (1998), *Strategic Issues in
nance*.

SWEDEN VS APA

The *Conter*
as an outlet
analyses o
improve th

Also in thi

Kalu, K.A.
Kimenyi, N
  Econom
Darkoh, M
  Sustain
Mainuddin
  Interac
Saitoti, G.
Mbaku, J.
  in the
Ngoh, V.J.
Udogu, E..
Magnarell
  Crimi
Mbaku, J.
Magnare
  Demo
Kimenyi,
  Micro

Sweden vs Apartheid

Putting Morality Ahead of Profit

ABDUL KARIM BANGURA
School of International Service
The American University, Washington DC, USA

ASHGATE

Published by
Ashgate Publishing Limited
Gower House
Croft Road
Aldershot
Hants GU11 3HR
England

Ashgate Publishing Company
Suite 420
101 Cherry Street
Burlington, VT 05401-4405
USA

Ashgate website: http://www.ashgate.com

British Library Cataloguing in Publication Data
Bangura, Abdul Karim, 1953-
    Sweden vs apartheid : putting morality ahead of profit. -
(Contemporary perspectives on developing societies)
    1. Apartheid 2. Sweden - Foreign relations - South Africa
    3. South Africa - Foreign relations - Sweden 4. Sweden -
Foreign relations - 1950- 5. South Africa - Foreign
relations - 20th century 6. Sweden - Politics and government
- 20th century
    I. Title
    327.4'85068

Library of Congress Cataloging-in-Publication Data
Bangura, Abdul Karim, 1953-
    Sweden vs apartheid : putting morality ahead of profit / Abdul Karim Bangura,
        p. cm. -- (Contemporary perspectives on developing societies)
    Includes bibliographical references and index.
    ISBN 0-7546-3684-4
    1. Sweden--Economic policy. 2. Sweden--Foreign relations--South Africa. 3. South
Africa--Foreign relations--Sweden. 4. Sweden--Foreign relations--Developing countries. 5.
Developing countries--Foreign relations--Sweden. 6. Developing countries--Economic
conditions. 7. Apartheid--South Africa. I. Title. II. Series.

HC375.B3295 2004
337.485068'09'045--dc22

ISBN 0 7546 3684 4

Printed and bound by Athenaeum Press, Ltd.,
Gateshead, Tyne & Wear.

Contents

Dedication

To the victims of Apartheid
To the memory of Olof Palme
To the Swedish taxpayer

Acknowledgements

I, and hopefully many readers, owe gratitude to:

Professors John Mukum Mbaku, Babalola Cole, William W. Ellis, Walter W. Hill, and Sulayman S. Nyang, for helpfully giving their time in reading the manuscript and offering constructive suggestions.

Professor Thomas Lundén, for supporting my research efforts during my studies at Stockholms Universitet in Sweden.

Shanelle Wells, for providing critical research and keyboarding assistance.

Diana Kelly, Fatmata Aminata Bangura, Isatu Ramatu Bangura and the other members of the various families to which I belong, for offering encouragement and displaying considerable forbearance.

Ali Kunda Bangura, my late father, for the courage of losing his life advocating the very issues about which I am presently concerned – freedom, justice and equality.

Fatmata Jalloh-Bangura, my mother, for providing the sense of assurance that such an endeavor could be successfully completed.

Duramany Deen-Sie Sawaneh and Abdul Rahman Kamara, for providing brotherly support during our studies at Stockholms Universitet in Sweden.

Professors, administrators and staff of American University's School of International Service, for providing stimulating academic nourishment.

American University students, for listening to and providing useful comments on the subject.

Preface

In contemporary international relations, the self-glorifying language is notoriously unflattering. What we often hear is a confusion of wealth with success, an obsession with being 'the sole superpower' and the 'profit motive,' and a plethora of bloody metaphors invoking images of Darwinian jungles and guerilla warfare. If we are to listen only to the supposedly self-glorifying rhetoric, we might well come away with the idea that international relations comprise a brutal battle for survival, devoid of rules, trust, or courtesies in which mercy and mutual consideration (much less altruism and concern for the public good) are sheer folly. Or, at best, we might come to believe that the aim of international relations is to join an exciting game, take risks and be challenged, get there ahead of the other country and, above all, 'have fun.' (It is worth mentioning that African languages do not have an exact translation for the Western notion of 'having fun,' and after adolescence an individual supposedly learns that risks and challenges can be foolish as well as invigorating, wasteful as well as productive.) Or, more cynically, international relations present themselves as a grueling necessity, without ultimate point or purpose. Strikingly lacking is a vision: the failure to see the 'global system' – except of course in flights of rhetoric about 'the magic of the capitalist world market' and 'the blessings of comparative advantage' that have very little to do with the actual on-the-job experience of most policy-makers and bureaucrats. In many such descriptions of international relations, we hear surprisingly little reference to respect for other peoples and cultures or shared prosperity. We read and hear about deadlines, organizational politics, moral mazes, 'tough' and sadistic leaders, carrot versus stick theories of motivation, international market pressures, and keeping ahead of the competition. As the larger vision gets lost from view, countries become so entrenched in their individual and increasingly isolated positions and ambitions that they lose sight of the purpose for living in an international community. It suffices to say that this is neither healthy and conducive to happiness and fulfillment for international relations, nor is it healthy and conducive to cooperation and efficiency in the world. Fortunately, there have been certain exceptions to this behavior. Indeed, Sweden's anti-Apartheid stance was one of them.

This book examines those factors that are thought to have dictated

Sweden's opposition to South Africa's Apartheid system (the official policies of political, social, cultural and economic discrimination and segregation enforced against non-whites in that country) and the nature of that opposition. There are many reasons why this book is significant. First, it examines the foreign policy 'posture' of a state that was once a great power (before World War I–in the sense that Sweden emerged as a major military power during the 16th Century and the early part of the 17th Century, enabling it to obtain control over some of the important trade routes to Russia and annexing several areas in Europe). Second, it looks at Sweden's neutrality policy which embraced the idea of international solidarity with weaker states and groups. Third, it serves as a valuable resource to those who teach comparative political analysis who, for one reason or the other, have not taken advantage of the many enriching examples available from Sweden. Fourth, it provides those readers who are not familiar with Sweden a descriptive account of the society's people, culture, manners and customs through the lenses of its political and economic policies, its organizations and institutions. Finally, the book is significant simply because it examines the policy of one of the first Western states (Sweden) that adopted an active anti-Apartheid stance when such a position was quite unpopular in the West.

The organization of the rest of this book is quite simple. Chapter 1 describes the scope of the problem, why the issue of Apartheid is the focus of the problem, and the major questions probed. Chapter 2 reviews the pertinent works that had examined various aspects of Sweden's dealings with South Africa during the Apartheid era. Chapter 3 examines Sweden's relations with the Third World for two major reasons: (1) to provide readers, especially those who are unfamiliar with Sweden's relations with the Third World, with a descriptive account of those relations; and (2) to find out whether or not certain assumptions can possibly be delineated from those relations that could be applied to Sweden's anti-Apartheid posture. Chapter 4 discusses those factors that shaped Sweden's anti-Apartheid policy. Chapter 5 is about the outcomes of the policy. Chapter 6 looks at the assassination of Olof Palme and the Apartheid regime's connection to it. Chapter 7 draws some conclusions. Finally, a postscript on the murder of Swedish Foreign Minister Anna Lindh was added after the manuscript was completed because she was Palme's protégée and an avid supporter of anti-Apartheid activities.

Chapter 1

General Introduction

Introduction

An examination of the key statements made by some Swedish government and non-government officials reveals that the Swedes took exception to South Africa's Apartheid system. The white minority rule, which was maintained in terms of races and on the massive exploitation of the blacks, was condemned in harsh language by the Swedes. Beginning with the 1960s, Apartheid received thorough criticisms from Swedish officials both in Sweden and the United Nations (UN). Because of their self-image as a people in solidarity with the disadvantaged countries and groups in the world, Swedes overwhelmingly supported any form of struggle in South Africa, and they were pleased with their country's assistance to the victims of Apartheid. On both moral and political grounds, many organizations in Sweden made known their disgust with the perils of Apartheid.

During the plenary meetings of the United Nations General Assembly (UNGA) of October 29, 1976, the Swedish Representative, His Excellency Olof Rydbeck, citing the fact that South Africa's so-called independent homelands or Bantustan policy was a convenient tool used by the Pretoria regime to consolidate white domination and continue the social and economic exploitation of black workers, made this scathing remark:

> The apartheid system–in whatever form–must be brought to an end. Over and over again it has been demonstrated how utterly false is the claim by the white regime that the apartheid policy can establish harmony and peace in South Africa. It is on the contrary, more evident than ever that all attempts to found a society on the principle of social discrimination are doomed to failure. The apartheid system, inhuman and morally repulsive as it is in its basic concept, is also inevitably a system of violence....(SIAS, 1997, p. 19).

In his statement to the United Nations Security Council (UNSC) on March 25, 1977, late Prime Minister Olof Palme of Sweden also rendered a scathing criticism on the system of Apartheid. Palme pointed out the racist tendencies of Apartheid, the Soweto Massacre that left 2,480 persons dead, the system of 'mental prisoners' that detained and exploited between 8,000 and 9,000 mentally-ill black Africans against their will for profit, the torture and deaths of political prisoners in South African jails, and how the Apartheid system dissolved family ties. Palme, therefore, asserted that Apartheid was a 'weird dictatorship of the minority for social and economic exploitation. But it also has a unique feature. Apartheid is the only tyranny branding a person right from birth according to the color of the skin. From the very moment of conception the child's destiny is determined. A Swedish author has called this system *spiritual genocide*' (SIAS, 1977, pp. 24-32).

Furthermore, warning that the actions taken at the UN or the lack of such actions could not serve as an excuse for being passive at the national level on the issue of Apartheid, Palme called on each country, each government, and each popular movement to embark upon the following actions:

1. Work for a halt to all arms sale to South Africa and all military cooperation with its government.

2. Seriously deal with the question of investment and export of capital to South Africa and Namibia (a country that was in South Africa's control).

3. Give material and political support to the liberation movements and the already autonomous states in the struggle for national independence and economic emancipation.

4. Refuse to recognize the so-called independent Bantustans–Transkei being the first–[to be] followed up by opposition to the efforts of international companies to give unofficial recognition by massive investments in those areas.

5. Increase the efforts to bring an end to the illegal occupation of Namibia by South Africa.

6. To set up parliamentary committees to investigate the activities of those companies which have subsidiaries in South Africa, for the purposes of ensuring that such companies are run on the lines of

internationally acknowledged working practices. Whereas these are not adhered to, the company should cease its activities entirely (SIAS, 1977, p. 32).

On March 29, 1977, Ambassador Andres I. Thunborg of Sweden, speaking at the UNSC, noted that all political parties in Sweden had taken the question of South Africa to be a major issue. Thunborg also maintained that Sweden was in full support of an internationally coordinated policy that would halt further foreign investments in South Africa. This was because he believed that Apartheid had a direct bearing on international peace and security (SIAS, 1977, pp. 33-36).

At the Maputo (Mozambique) Conference held on May 19, 1977, Ola Ullsten, the Swedish Minister of International Development Cooperation, voicing his disappointment with the UNSC for its failure to consider steps that would have inhibited further investment in South Africa, asserted the following:

> South Africa itself and the abhorrent system of apartheid is not formally on the agenda of this Conference. But as long as apartheid exists the South African regime will play a crucial role in the development of the situation in the whole of Southern Africa (SIAS, 1977, p. 39).

Also, at the same Maputo Conference, Palme, on May 20, 1977, put the case of Apartheid squarely on the laps of the Western nations. He suggested that the Western nations were being tested on both moral grounds and the civilization which they claim to champion because of their failure to abolish a vicious doctrine (Apartheid) that thrived on racism. Palme, therefore, concluded that 'as long as there is apartheid and racism, there can be no peace' (SIAS, 1977, pp. 43-53).

However, as suggested earlier, such scathing criticisms of South Africa's Apartheid system did not come from Swedish government officials alone. Swedish trade union movements, for example, were for many years in the forefront of the struggle to end Apartheid.

In a 1975 report written by a study delegation of the Swedish Trade Union Confederation (LO) and the Central Organization of Salaried Employees in Sweden (TCO) that toured South Africa, it was emphasized that these movements strongly detested Apartheid and the social system in South Africa. They, therefore, called upon all organizations as well as the Swedish public to join in a common cause to support the struggle against the Pretoria government. These labor movements specifically demanded that there be the following:

> restrictions in the Swedish rules for capital transfers to South Africa as to prevent new Swedish investments in the country as long as the Swedish enterprises are profiting by the Black, Asiatic and Coloured labor force through discriminating working conditions (LO/TCO, 1975, preface).

It is quite obvious from these statements that Sweden would have liked to see an end to Apartheid in South Africa, bring South Africa under African majority rule, and render obsolete the possibility of a potential international crisis is Southern Africa. But such assumptions leave unanswered many important questions. For example, why did the Swedish government not pass a legislation that could have facilitated the complete withdrawal of Swedish companies operating in South Africa? Also, if the Swedish government believed in its call that the way to eradicate Apartheid was by isolating South Africa, why did Sweden not begin by breaking off diplomatic relations with South Africa. However, as an LO/TCO report maintained, it was highly held in the Swedish Parliament that isolated Swedish actions would have been contrary to 'realistic politics' (LO/TCO, 1975, p. 110).

Indeed, the preceding questions are so difficult that it will not be easy to provide all of the possible answers for them. As a matter of fact, the complexity of human affairs makes such a task herculean. What one can hope for is that this book challenges some of the suggestions that had been made in either discussing or analyzing the issue of Apartheid in South Africa.

Issue as the Focus of the Problem

Politics is made up of many fundamental issues, and they serve as the link between countries and generations. K. J. Holsti (1991, p. 176) captured this sentiment succinctly when he stated that 'issues after all are the stuff of politics.' Thus, it is safe to suggest that foreign policies vary with the type of issue or what James N. Rosenau called 'issue areas.' He defined these as follows:

> (1) a cluster of values, the allocation or the potential allocation of which (2) leads the affected or potentially affected actors to differ so greatly over (a) the way in which the values should be allocated or (b) the horizontal levels at which the values should authorize that (3) they engage in distinctive behavior designed to mobilize support for the attainment of their particular values (Holsti, 1971, pp. 17-18).

Thus, from its title, it can be noted that this book is issue-oriented. The issue that is being examined here is Apartheid, an issue that was not confined within the borders of South Africa. It was international in its scope and, therefore, should be treated on that level of analysis.

As the United Nations Association of the United States (UN-USA) correctly observed, South Africa's Apartheid system was a major issue before the UN. South Africa's racial policies first became the UN's business in 1946, when South Africans of Indian descent lodged a protest against that country's discriminatory legislation. Apartheid as an issue made its first appearance before the UNGA in 1952 (Puchala, 1981, p. 37)–i.e. four years after the Nationalist Party of South Africa assumed political power and codified Apartheid as the official system of the state in 1948 (for details, see Kunnie, 2000, p. 18). And even though the South African regime continued to charge the UN with interfering into its internal affairs, South Africa faced harsh condemnation at the organization's sessions. As a matter of fact, a committee (the Special Committee Against Apartheid) was formed to coordinate efforts and mobilize international opinion against Apartheid, and questions on South Africa's racial policies were for many years raised before the UNSC (Puchala, 1981, pp. 37-41). Given this backdrop, how can Sweden's position on the issue of Apartheid be examined? In short, what questions are plausible in examining such a position?

Apartheid, like many other issues, had its staunch supporters and ardent opponents. And the objective in this book is to examine the ambitions of one of Apartheid's many opponents (Sweden) to change the status quo in South Africa by supporting the liberation struggle against the Pretoria regime. Thus, the major questions of this book are as follows:

1. To what extent was Sweden supporting the anti-Apartheid movement (the liberation struggle against the minority regime in South Africa), and how can that support be characterized?

2. What factors underlay that support? Put differently, how was that support related to those vital factors thought to have influenced or affected Sweden's foreign policy outcome on the issue of Apartheid?

3. What was different and/or similar about Sweden's perception of Apartheid and its consequences on international politics vis-a-vis those of the super-powers at the time–i.e. the United States (US) and the Union of Soviet Socialist Republics (USSR)?

While contemplating these questions, it will be useful, at this point, to review the relevant works that have dealt with some aspects of Sweden's relations with South Africa to ferret out the available suggestions. Before doing so, however, it makes sense to conclude this chapter with a brief discussion of how Sweden is governed at the national level for those readers who may not be familiar with the way national political decisions are made in the country.

How Sweden is Governed at the National Level: A Synopsis

Following a revolt in which the army played a major role, the autocratic King Gustaf IV Adolf of Sweden was imprisoned and subsequently deposed on March 13, 1908. Heavy losses that resulted from an ill-fated war sparked the revolt. The King was blamed for his inability to defend the nation. A year later, Jean Bernadotte, a French field marshal, acceded to the Swedish throne after a series of maneuvers that led to a coup d'etat. Bernadotte was one of Napoleon Bonaparte's most able commanders. The accession of the new monarch led to the creation of a new constitution and a change in the form of government. The most important constitutional document was the Instrument of Government, dating back to June 6, 1809. This is now Sweden's Flag Day–a kind of semi-official commemoration day. The document laid down the constitutional powers of the King, the government and Parliament (Riksdag) (Wadensjö, 1979, p. 81).

The other constitutional documents–the Parliament Act, the Act of Succession, and the Freedom of the Press Act–established the composition, procedures and sessions of Parliament, the rights of succession within the new royal family and the general procedures relating to the freedom of the press. The new constitution provided for a more democratic form of government, albeit parliamentary representation remained highly undemocratic. The nobility and the church, which made up only a small minority of the population, were each represented in a parliament composed of four estates (Nobility, Church, Burghers and the Peasant). Each estate had one vote in Parliament. In essence, the Swedish peasants who made up the overwhelming majority of the population only had one-quarter of the votes in Parliament. Even though absolute monarchy had been abolished, the new constitution continued to grant excessive powers to the King. The monarch was responsible for the appointment of the government, and the government in turn was responsible to Parliament. However, since the latter seldom met (initially, every fifth year), its influence was minimal. In 1866, the Estates Parliament was replaced by a bicameral parliament, although its powers were quite restricted (Wadensjö, 1979, p. 81).

By the mid-1950s, the Swedish constitution of 1809 and the parliamentary statutes had become obsolete. A regular practice developed alongside the provisions of the constitution which in many instances reduced the latter to a mere formality. To comply with the demand for a modernization of the constitution, a Commission of Enquiry was appointed in 1955. The commission called for the replacement in 1970 of the bicameral parliament by a unicameral one comprising 350 members elected by proportional representation. (Weibull, 1980, p. 64)

Lengthy negotiations led to a new constitution that was adopted by the parliament in 1974 and took effect the following year. The constitution stipulated that all powers derive from the people. Consequently, the powers of the King were reduced to purely ceremonial ones. Thus, the number of seats in Parliament was also reduced by one–from 350 to 349. The Speaker of Parliament took over the task of the King in presiding over the formation of new governments. Instead of the King, the Prime Minister serves as the chairman at the government's meetings. The King can attend these meetings only when the government invites him on special occasions (Weibull, 1980, pp. 64-5).

When King Gustav VI Adolf died in 1973, he was succeeded by his grandson, Carl XVI Gustaf. Realizing the gender bias in the succession rules, Parliament in 1979 passed the Act of Succession, giving women the same right to inherit the throne, effective from January 1980. This means that the King's first child, Princess Victoria, now becomes heir to the throne, instead of her younger brother, Carl Philip (Weibull, 1980, pp. 65-6).

The government exercises executive power in Sweden. Its most important functions include presenting new legislation, putting forward budget proposals, and issuing statutes. The government and particularly the Ministry of Foreign Affairs is also responsible for maintaining the nation's international relations. The government appoints senior administrators and military officers. In addition, it can adjudicate in issues dealing with individual appeals from other government authorities (Wadensjö, 1979, pp. 84-5).

The Prime Minister is the head of government. He is assisted by a number of cabinet ministers, most of whom head their respective ministries. The remaining ministers are either ministers without portfolio who are responsible for certain specific policy areas within a ministry or coordinate policy issues that concern several ministries. Examples of such policy issues include school policy questions within the Ministry of Education, foreign aid issues within the Ministry of Foreign Affairs and energy policy questions within the Ministry of Industry. Government ministries in Sweden are relatively small units with approximately 100 persons, including clerical staff, in each ministry. The administration of government policy is carried out by the Central Administrative Boards which are relatively independent vis-à-vis government ministries. The different government ministries are divided into separate departments, each with its own department head. The Under Secretary of State, who is the official closest to a minister, is one of the few political appointees in a ministry–i.e. s/he belongs to the same political party as the minister and usually resigns with the minister when there is a change in government. The Under Secretary of State is responsible for political work within the ministry. Other senior officials in a ministry include the Permanent Secretary who supervises the formal process of administrative decision-making and the Chief Legal Officer who actually drafts legislation (Wadensjö, 1979, pp. 85-6).

Although individual members of government make decisions, the cabinet as a whole is responsible for all government decisions. Once a week, formal government decisions are made at the government building called the Chancery Building. During these half-hour cabinet meetings, which are presided over by the Prime Minister, the hundreds of decisions made are not discussed. These government decisions would have already been discussed by the entire government at plenary cabinet meetings that are usually held twice a week under the chairmanship of the Prime Minister. Government decisions are also made informally at cabinet luncheons in the private restaurant in the Chancery Building. These luncheons allow cabinet members to meet regularly in a relaxed atmosphere behind closed doors (Wadensjö, 1979, p. 86).

The initiative for a legislation can be taken by Parliament in the form of a parliamentary motion or by the government directly. To investigate a particular issue, the government appoints a committee of commission of inquiry comprised of members of Parliament from both government and opposition parties, as well as non-political experts. After a thorough investigation that may last for several years, the committee or commission could recommend proposals for policy action requiring new legislation. These policy proposals are then sent to governmental and non-governmental agencies for their feedback. After considering the comments, the government could formulate a final legislative proposal in the form of a bill and present it to Parliament for action (Wadensjö, 1979, p. 87).

Popular sovereignty in Sweden hinges upon the principles of universal and equal suffrage, within the framework of a representative parliamentary form of government. Parliamentary elections are held on the third Sunday in September every three years. Voter turnout is generally high, with approximately 90 percent of the eligible voters registering their choices. All Swedish citizens who 18 years or older are eligible to vote and run for office.

Of the 349 seats in Parliament, 310 are constituency seats; the rest are equalization seats. The former are based on county boundaries, and the latter are distributed according to the total number of votes each political party receives. A party must receive at least four percent of the total number of votes to be eligible for the equalization seats. Nonetheless, a party that garners at least 12 percent of the total number of votes cast in an individual constituency will be eligible for the allocation of seats, even though it does not meet the four percent criterion (Wadensjö, 1979, pp. 87-8).

All newly elected representatives assemble for the first session of Parliament. During this session, the Prime Minister presents the government's policy declaration. Parliament is in session from the October 1st until May 31st. In January of each year, the government presents its budget for the subsequent fiscal year. During the 15 days following the submission of the budget for debate in committee, individual members or groups in parliament can introduce their own motions. The major parliamentary motions are usually put forward by the opposition parties. Members of Parliament can attach amendments to all government bills. It is customary for the presentation of government bills to be followed by a debate in parliament. The major parliamentary debate is the 'general political debate' held shortly after the beginning of the fall session of parliament and the debate on the budget that follows its submission to various standing committees. Major foreign policy debates are also held in Parliament (Wadensjö, 1979, p. 89).

Parliamentary motions are subsequently debated in committees. There are 16 standing committees, each of which has 15 members selected in proportion to party representation in Parliament. Each committee has its own secretariat and special advisers. The majority of the members of Parliament serve on committees as either permanent or deputy members. Occasionally, special committees are also appointed. The most important part of parliamentary work is carried out in committees where government bills are thoroughly scrutinized. The committees subsequently report back to Parliament which, following consideration of the committees' deliberations, may either approve or reject the proposals. Committees meetings are held on Tuesdays, Thursdays and Fridays; plenary sessions are held on Wednesdays when the entire Parliament is assembled for discussion and voting. The Speaker chairs the plenary sessions. S/he is assisted by three Deputy Speakers. It is during Speaker's conferences that the planning of parliamentary sessions, the order in which questions are taken, the drawing up of lists of speakers, etc. are discussed (Wadensjö, 1979, p. 90).

Parliament has tax-raising powers and legislative authority. However, it does not generally make large-scale changes in the government's taxation proposals. The major expenditure items are dependent on past reform legislation in areas such as pensions, child allowances and civil servants' wages which hardly any political party would be willing to reduce. Parliament can also scrutinize the conduct of government and public administration. A member of parliament can put an interpellation or parliamentary question to a cabinet minister in matters dealing with his area of responsibility. In the case of an answer to an interpellation, parliament can debate a minister's handling of the issue in question. However, an answer to a parliamentary question cannot be debated. The Standing Committee on the Constitution deals with the scrutiny of governmental activities on the basis of the available official papers. In the event that a government minister is censured by a committee and the majority in Parliament votes in favor, the minister in question would have to resign. If the Prime Minister faces a similar fate, the entire government would have to resign (Wadensjö, 1969, p. 90-1).

Civil servants are subject to parliamentary control through the offices of four Parliamentary Ombudsmen appointed by Parliament. Citizens can consult the ombudsmen for redress if they perceive government authorities of treating them unfairly. On behalf of Parliament, parliamentary auditors can examine the way government revenues are used. The National Audit Board is responsible for the thorough investigation of government finances. Civil servants can also be scrutinized by the Chancellor of Justice (Wadensjö, 1979, p. 91).

Central Administrative Boards, which are relatively independent, are responsible for the administration of governmental and parliamentary decisions. Each of the central agencies has its own Director General who together with a number of senior officials and laymen form a board. Appointed by the government, the laymen are drawn from organizations and civic bodies that have an interest in a board's area of operation. The Director Generals are appointed by the government, usually on political grounds, for a period of six years. Examples of these Boards are the National Board of Health and Welfare which deals with social and medical issues, the National Board of Education which handles the supervision of the Swedish school system and the Labor Market Board which implements labor market policy. The majority of the Boards are situated in Stockholm. However, in order to provide employment opportunities in other parts of the country, some of work of the Boards has been moved to those areas (Wadensjö, 1979, pp. 91-2).

Chapter 2

Perspectives on Sweden's Foreign Policy toward South Africa

While, to the best of my knowledge, no published work exists that has dealt exclusively with Sweden's foreign policy toward South Africa in its entirety, there are, nevertheless, certain works that had examined various aspects of Sweden's dealings with South Africa either in a Southern Africa regional perspective, in a Third World perspective, or in a global context. The majority of these works was published in the 1970s and 1980s, while three of them were all published in 1999. In reviewing these works, one is confronted, over and over again, with a recurring theme: the Swedish policy of 'caution' toward South Africa—that is, Sweden severely condemned the policies of Apartheid, but it was not willing to suffer a serious economic loss in its dealings with South Africa.

In 1974, Ake Magnusson, in his monograph, *Swedish Investments in South Africa* (a condensed version of a survey on Swedish companies and their investments in South Africa), set the tone on the policy of 'caution.' After sending out a questionnaire to some 60 Swedish companies, the author found that, even though South Africa was of 'secondary importance' in Swedish foreign trade, it did not imply that South Africa was of no importance to Sweden. This was due to the fact that Swedes who worked for companies that did business with South Africa lived quite pleasant lives. Thus, while the Swedish employer might have detested Apartheid, he, nevertheless, in an indirect manner, supported the system by his presence in South Africa. Hence, Magnusson suggested that although the LO/TCO and the Swedish Ecumenical Council had urged Swedish companies to rectify the disparities between their white and non-white workers in South Africa, these companies had been cautious in implementing such decisive measures.

A year later (in 1975), the caution theme was picked up by an LO/TCO study. This study maintained that, even though the Swedish government took exception to Apartheid, many officials in government circles believed that isolated Swedish actions against South Africa would be counter-productive for Sweden in realist politics. Thus, Sweden had been cautious by trying to avoid actions that would prove to be short-lived and ineffective.

In 1977, the Scandinavian Institute of African Studies in its own monograph, *Nordic Statements on Apartheid*, presented a series of speeches by Swedish and other Scandinavian officials at the UNGA, the UNSC and the UN conference in Maputo held during the same year. The underlying theme of this work was that the initiatives and actions of Sweden and the other Scandinavian states were to make possible universal condemnation and eventual elimination of Apartheid, as long as Cold War considerations were avoided.

A series of essays by various authors that focused on the relations between the Scandinavian countries and those of Southern Africa, in the book edited by Douglas Anglin, et. al., *Canada, Scandinavia and Southern Africa*, was published in 1978. These essays purported the idea that Sweden's foreign policy toward South Africa was one of caution. For example, in examining the issue of the Scandinavian states and the arms embargo, Abdul S. Minty suggested that the failure of the Swedish government to close a loophole by having weak control over the production and sales of companies made it easy for South Africa to buy Swedish arms through subsidiaries such as Asea in South Africa. Thus, even though Sweden had one of the strict regulations on the arms embargo, it had been cautious not to upset the dealings of Swedish companies doing business in South Africa.

In that same book, Roger Leys' essay, 'Scandinavian Development Assistance to Botswana, Lesotho and Swaziland,' suggested that, while Sweden and the other Scandinavian states had provided 'humanitarian' assistance to the front-line states, certain ambiguities and inconsistencies existed in the assistance. For example, he noted that the 'progressive' image of hostility toward Apartheid by the Scandinavian states was not at par with the limited amount of development aid given to the front-line states (countries that sought to oppose Apartheid). Furthermore, Leys noted that there existed a wider problem with the consistency of material and diplomatic support to the front-line states in their anti-Apartheid efforts.

Also, Thorvald Stotenberg, in his treatise on 'Nordic Opportunities and Responsibilities in Southern Africa' (in Anglin, 1978) propounded the idea that while there was no disagreement among responsible Swedish and other Scandinavian politicians about the ills of the Apartheid system, these politicians, nonetheless, were not willing to sacrifice jobs to facilitate an effective economic boycott of South Africa. Stotenberg even predicted that this cautious attitude among Scandinavian politicians would never change.

Furthermore, in his essay, 'Nordic Policy trends Towards South Africa' (in

Anglin, 1978), Anders Thonberg submitted the idea that, even when Sweden proposed at the UNGA in 1976 that the Security Council take necessary steps to stop foreign investments in South Africa, very little action had been taken either by Sweden or other Capitalist nations, in spite of the fact that the proposition was passed.

In addition to that, Mai Palmberg, writing on 'Present Imperialist Policies in Southern Africa: The Case for Scandinavian Disassociation' (in Anglin, 1978), maintained that Sweden and the other Scandinavian states had been in the forefront among the Capitalist states that gave support to the liberation struggle against South Africa. Palmberg added that these countries had obtained a reputation for being on the side of the liberation struggle in the UN and other international contexts. And that while most of the support for the liberation groups had come from the Socialist and African states, the Scandinavian support had nonetheless been quite significant. Furthermore, the author contended that, even though the Scandinavian aid to the liberation forces could be termed as a *de facto* recognition of the legitimacy of the groups involved, the effort was often based on the idea that the solution of the problems in South Africa laid in the hands of the United States and its allies.

In his monograph, *Policy Issues and Economic Sanctions on South Africa*, published in 1981, D. G. Clarke proposed that Sweden's policy to prohibit new investments by Swedish-domiciled corporate groups had been a weak attempt at absolutism by the Swedish state. He rendered this proposition after a careful review of the exemptions in Sweden's prohibition policy. These exemptions were specifically designed as a caution to avoid income losses and unemployment in Sweden.

Finally, in 1982, Lars Rudebeck, writing on 'Nordic Policies Toward the Third World,' in the book edited by Bengt Sundelius, *Foreign Policies of Northern Europe* (1982), suggested that, because of Sweden's close ties with the Capitalist world, its policies toward the Third World did not differ much from those of other Capitalist states. But he also pointed out the fact that Sweden's aid policies had been 'progressive' compared to those of the other Capitalist states–that is, aid had been given to radical regimes and national liberation forces in Southern Africa.

In addition to the preceding works, there also exists a body of literature that briefly discussed Sweden's response to the South African problem–that is because the major foci of these studies are on Sweden's 'government and politics' and Sweden's 'foreign relations' in general. For example, in the book entitled *Sweden and the United Nations* (1956), the Swedish Institute of International Affairs, in examining Sweden's role in the UN on the South African question, presented Sweden's position on the race conflict in that country (i.e. South Africa). According to the institute, Sweden, beginning with the earlier discussions on South Africa's race conflict in 1952, took a firm position on bringing to light the perils of the South African race problem at the UN. Sweden argued that Article 2 (7), which prohibits the UN from intervening in questions which fall essentially within a given state's jurisdiction, should not have prevented the Organization from discussing issues on human rights abuse. Noting that the term 'domestic jurisdiction' was relative and that its meaning had changed in proportion to developments in the field of international law and international relations, Swedish officials, therefore, argued that the South African race conflict should be looked at within the same vein as the UN's investigation of the existence of forced labor in various countries at the time.

In 1976, Nils Andrén, in his *Power-Balance and Non-Alignment*, maintained that Sweden pursued a policy of 'dualism' toward South Africa: that is, on the one hand, Swedish public opinion had sustained the effort to expose at home the viciousness of the Apartheid system and the plight of the 'colored' and 'Negro' groups–thus, strong and nationwide organizations supported the anti-Apartheid campaign which also enjoyed some 'cautious' support from the Swedish government; on the other hand, Swedish firms were enjoying profitable investments in the expanding South African economy. Andrén, therefore, argued that Sweden's official activity in relation to South Africa primarily consisted of public statements against the Apartheid system and support for UN recommendations against that system. However, Andrén presented no empirical evidence to support his assumptions.

In 1977, Kenneth Hermele and Karl-Anders Larsson, in their famous book, *Solidaritet eller Imperialism*, presented a somewhat similar view to that of Andrén's. By positing that Sweden's relations with the Third World appeared double faced (i.e. on the one hand, Sweden's policies toward the Third World would not differ much from those of other Capitalist states if its basic economic interests were to be threatened; on the other hand, Swedish aid policies has had a progressive profile. Hermele and Larsson saw Sweden's position on the South African question within similar purview: that is, on the one hand, Sweden's investments in South Africa continued; on the other hand, Sweden provided humanitarian assistance to the victims of Apartheid and those liberation forces that sought to change the status-quo in South Africa.

In 1999, Tom Sellström continued the caution theme in three of his companion volumes: *Sweden and National Liberation in Southern Africa: Formation of a Popular Opinion (1950-1970)*, *Sweden and National Liberation in Souther Africa: A concerned partnership (1970-1994)*, and *Liberation in Southern Africa–Regional and Swedish Voices: Interviews from Angola,*

Mozambique, Zimbabwe, Namibia, South Africa, the Front-line and Sweden.
In these books, Sellström documented the involvement of Sweden in the
liberation struggle in Southern Africa, utilizing source material at government
and non-government organization (NGO) archives and interviews with key
actors in Sweden and Southern Africa. The author also examined the social,
political, and economic factors that helped to shape Sweden's involvement in
the anti-Apartheid struggle.

The preceding review brings to mind the following words of wisdom from
poet Edna St. Vincent Millay:

> ... Upon this gifted age, in its dark hour rains from the sky a meteoric shower of
> facts. They lie unquestioned, uncombined. Wisdom enough to teach us of our ills
> is daily spun, but there exists no loom to weave it into fabric (Millay, 1956, p. 697).

As it can be surmised from the preceding excerpt, the task in the current book
is to weave the fabric of the accumulated wisdom from this research on the
loom of levels/units of analysis.

Chapter 3

Sweden and the Third World

The objective of this chapter is twofold: (1) to provide readers, especially those who are unfamiliar with Sweden's relations with the Third World, with a descriptive account of those relations; and (2) to find out whether or not certain assumptions can possibly be delineated from those relations that could be applied to Sweden's anti-Apartheid posture. But before the discussion on Sweden's relations with the Third World is delved into, a revelation of the bias in this chapter is in order.

Like many other studies that have dealt with the relations between the richer states and the Third World, this chapter also treats the Third World more as an object of Sweden's foreign policies. Such an approach simply reflects the fact that it was not until the mid-1970s that the Third World began to have an active voice in international affairs. Robert Mortimer captured this truism quite well when he stated:

> Weak states never have had much say in world politics. Accordingly, the developing states of Asia, Africa, and South America have been more objects than subjects in the international system. Until quite recently, to speak of the Third World in international politics was to identify an arena of great-power competition, not an actor. Only in the 1970s has a new collective actor begun to give an active role to the Third World in international affairs (Mortimer, 1984, p. 1).

Here, Third World countries are discussed as a group because they are the formerly colonized or semi-colonized countries of Africa, Asia, Central and South America. They are generally opposed to colonialism and capitalist-imperialism. The common bond that ties these states together is the fact that they are poor and, thus, occupy the bottom position on the international economic totem-pole. As a major UN spokesman for the Third World, Mahbub ul Haq, put it:

> A poverty curtain has descended right across the face of our world, dividing it materially and philosophically into two separate planets, two unequal humanities–one embarrassingly rich and the other desperately poor (Mortimer, 1984 and Mahbub ul Haq, 1976, p. 15).

With this prelude, an examination of the policies and activities of Sweden with regard to the countries of the Third World can now be embarked upon.

In his book on the Scandinavian states' policies toward the Third World, Rudebeck suggested that those policies generally involved actions of the states themselves, or they might cover policies carried out by industrial and business co-operations, banks and trade unions. And quite appropriately, four areas of inquiry always dominated the discussion on Sweden's relations with the Third World. These areas are: (1) trade, (2) investments, (3) development co-operation, and (4) political issues (Rudebeck, 1982, p. 143). This book, hence, follows this folklore of inquiry.

Trade With the Third World

Like many other industrialized states in the world, Sweden is not remit from those states' dependence on foreign trade. Sweden has a reasonably large number of transnational corporations that have done quite well in circumventing tariff barriers. Nonetheless, other factors such as financial aid for the establishment of branch companies, low wages and better market opportunities have over time given a helping hand to Sweden's foreign trade success story (Wadensjö, 1979, p. 109).

And representing only about 12 per cent of its total foreign trade, Sweden's trade with the Third World has over time been dominated by oil and petroleum products from the developing countries. The second largest group of products imported by Sweden from the Third World is that of food stuffs–this group of products include coffee, tea, cocoa and spices. These goods are imported because they cannot be competitively produced in Sweden. Imports of industrial products, on the other hand, are relatively small but had been growing at a rapid pace–especially ready-made garments (Swedish Secretariat for Future Studies, 1979, pp. 25-26).

A breakdown of total imports from the developing countries in 1975, for example, revealed that Brazil, Hong Kong, Iran, Nigeria, Saudi Arabia, and the United Arab Emirates combined for an aggregate of about 50 per cent of Sweden's imports from the Third World. It was estimated that if Colombia, Kuwait, Qatar, South Korea and Taiwan were included, these countries together would have accounted for more than 70 per cent of Swedish imports from the Third World in 1975 (Swedish Secretariat for Future Studies, 1979, p. 27).

At about 69 per cent of its total exports to the underdeveloped countries, Sweden's industrial products (especially machinery, transport equipment and manufactured goods) dominated that aspect of its trade with the Third World. Raw materials (a few isolated commodities like pulp, iron ore and aid shipments of grain) represented only about seven percent of Sweden's total exports to the underdeveloped states. Unlike its imports from Third World countries, Sweden's exports to those states were widely distributed. In 1975, Algeria, Brazil, Iran, Iraq and Liberia emerged as the biggest markets for Swedish goods in the Third World, accounting for almost 37 per cent of Swedish exports. The other major recipients of Swedish goods in the Third World during the same year included India, Mexico, Peru and Saudi Arabia, which together received 18 per cent of those exports (Swedish Secretariat for Future Studies, 1979, pp. 27-28).

Of importance is the fact that except for Colombia, the largest Third World exporters to Sweden were oil-producing states and the Newly Industrializing Countries (NICs). All of these states belonged to the 'upper class' or 'middle class' among the Third World countries. In essence, Sweden bought very little indeed from the poorest states in the Third World (Swedish Secretariat for Future Studies, 1979, p. 29).

As far as exports were concerned, oil-producing states aside, those Third World countries where Swedish industrial companies had manufacturing subsidiaries emerged as the largest recipients of Swedish products (Swedish Secretariat for Future Studies, 1979, p. 29). However, despite the fact that Sweden's trade with the Third World comprised only a small fraction of its (Sweden) total foreign trade, the trade was, nonetheless, important to the Swedes. As Rudebeck asserted,

> Third World export markets are relatively more important for Sweden than for the other Nordic countries, at least in a quantitative sense. This is indicated by the fact that with only 37 per cent of the Nordic countries' total population of about 22 million people, Sweden accounts, on an average, for close to half of the value of Nordic exports to the Third World (Rudebeck, 1982, p. 144).

As will be seen later in this book, this situation has enabled Sweden to take a leading role among the Nordic countries in responding to the needs of African and other Third World countries.

Investments in the Third World

Compared to the growth of its internal investments (whereas its gross investments exclusive of housing rose, for example, by 65 per cent in current prices between 1972 and 1977), Sweden's foreign investments were growing rapidly–for example, Swedish foreign investments grew by about 125 per cent between 1972 and 1979. Swedish investments in the Third World rose by about 280 per cent between 1972 and 1977 alone. In some of the Third World countries, Sweden's investments grew even greater. In the case of Brazil, for example, Swedish investments in that country rose ten-fold (i.e. by about 1,000 per cent) between 1972 and 1977 (Swedish Secretariat for Future Studies, 1979, pp. 30-31).

And as Rudebeck pointed out, although the officially registered annual flows of capital from the Scandinavian states to Third World countries were quite small, Sweden was by far the largest investor in those countries. By 1977, Sweden's flows to the underdeveloped countries reached 0.99 per cent of its GNP–this figure included direct investments, export credits and international lending by Swedish banks (Rudebeck, 1982, p. 149).

From 1960 to 1974, especially, Third World countries increased their share of Sweden's manufacturing goods that went abroad. But a great deal of the increase took place in Latin America, while shares for Africa and Asia combined actually declined (in relative terms, but not in absolute terms). And the largest share of Sweden's investments in the Third World went to Brazil during this same period. The reason for this, according to Rudebeck, was the fact that during 1970-1972, 52 per cent of all permissions for Swedish investment capital overseas was earmarked for Brazil. Thus, about 65 per cent of all persons employed by Swedish subsidiary companies in underdeveloped countries were in Brazil. Yet, when the total amount of Swedish foreign investments is looked at, the Brazilian investments represented only 2.4 percent of those investments. In essence, while Sweden's involvement in the international and, therefore, developing economies was large relative to its small population base, it was, nonetheless, small in absolute terms (Rudebeck, 1982, pp. 151-154).

In addition, according to Rudebeck, Sweden's interests in the Brazilian economy could be traced back to the 19th Century after the founding of trading agencies by Swedish firms. And that even though Swedish companies did not begin manufacturing in Brazil until the last 20 years of the 20th Century, the rapid expansion of those Swedish companies, however, began to take shape immediately after World War II. And as Rudebeck further noted, Swedish manufacturing companies in Brazil were not different from other transnational corporations as far as high social costs for the host country, use of intensive technology that did little to resolve the unemployment problem, the creation of technological dependence, and the contribution to balance-of-payments problems that often went with importing from parent companies were concerned. Furthermore, he suggested, Brazil's military dictatorship of the 1960s and 1970s, which favored a capitalist development strategy, was ideal for creating a particularly favorable market atmosphere for private investors from Sweden and other industrialized countries as well (Rudebeck, 1982, pp. 154).

Development Cooperation with the Third World

'Development aid,' asserted Rudebeck, 'is not by any means the most important type of Third World policy in a quantitative sense. Other flows of resources and capital are much more important when added together. Sweden, Norway, and Denmark are among the world's major donors of development aid in relation to their gross national products (GNPs). Sweden is even number one among the developed capitalist countries' (Rudebeck, 1982, p. 155). But as to be seen here, and the discussion ahead on aid, Sweden's rise to its number one position in terms of aid given as a percentage of its GNP is not at all haphazard. It was an outcome of a series of policies designed to address the rudiments of poverty in the Third World.

When Sweden embarked upon its role as aid-donor (on a larger scale, of course–the Swedish bilateral aid program was initially launched in 1952 when the Central Committee for Swedish Technical Assistance to Less Developed Countries was created) in the early 1960s, a major question loomed as to which strategy it should use in disbursing its aid to the developing countries. The question had to do with whether Sweden should embark upon a bilateral approach (that is, aid given directly to the states) or a multilateral approach (that is, aid given to the various branches of the UN or other international organizations). During this period (1960s), the multilateral approach was favored for both practical and ideological reasons. On the practical level, Sweden lacked the administrative capacity to channel very much of its aid. And on the ideological level, there existed a pro-UN sentiment as being proper and progressive (Rudebeck, 1982, p. 157).

Combined with its 'multilateralist ethic' (Beckman, 1978, p. 24) was its legacy from the *folkrorelser*, according to Joseph Board, 'a strong undercurrent of morality in Swedish political life, which exists alongside an equally characteristic sense of realism. Sweden is a wealthy country, and many Swedes feel deeply that wealth carries with it an obligation to improve the position of the less fortunately endowed.' Thus, Board suggested, Sweden's official foreign aid which amounted to only 45 million Kronor by 1961 increased to well over 400 million Kronor by 1968 (an almost tenfold jump). In addition to that, there was strong pressure on the Swedish government to increase its aid to one per cent of its GNP (Board, 1970, p. 202).

During the 1960s, Sweden's aid to the Third World states was not large (in absolute terms) when compared to the aid that was coming from the USA or when measured against the needs of the recipient countries. Swedish aid, nevertheless, carried with it a symbolic value that was larger in proportion to its size. This was due to the fact that Sweden was non-aligned during the Cold War, and because it never participated in the European scramble for colonies. Thus, Sweden had a considerably greater degree of freedom in its choice of aid-recipients than did the larger powers (Board, 1970, pp. 202-203).

But even though Sweden, in the 1960s, preferred multilateral aid without political strings, almost half of its aid was bilateral in nature. This was because Sweden wanted to establish closer relationships with the Third World and, therefore, most of its bilateral aid was in the form of technical and educational assistance as opposed to credits or grants-in-kind. The list of countries that emerged as major recipients of the aid (some of the aid jointly administered with other Scandinavian states) included Ethiopia, India, Kenya, Liberia, Pakistan, Tanzania and Tunisia. Few direct grants, such as Swedish paper for India's school books, and a few cases of credits were officially tied to a 'buy Swedish' policy as contracts usually went to Swedish firms especially in those areas where Swedish industry excelled. One of the more important contributions made by the Swedish aid was in the area of family planning, an issue that encountered far fewer domestic political problems in Sweden than, say, in the United States (Board, 1970, p. 203).

By the 1970s, however, Sweden's emphasis on development co-operation shifted from that of multilateralism to one of bilateralism. The Swedish International Development Authority (SIDA) expanded and developed its own vested interests in the development promotion effort. Furthermore, the total aid increased and, thereby, became more important in Swedish national politics and economics (Rudebeck, 1982, p. 157).

Two reasons, as Rudebeck suggested, were responsible for the shift of emphasis in Sweden's development cooperation: (1) Swedish aid-administrators were dismayed by the fact that UN aid had become too bureaucratic and cumbersome, and (2) an extensive debate emerged on the selection of recipients. It was opined by many Swedes, especially the radicals within the Social Democratic Party (which was still in power at the time), that

Swedish aid could be better utilized by those countries with political regimes that were willing to respond to the official aspirations of the Swedish development program. These aspirations were, and continue to be: (a) 'economic and social equalization,' (b) 'change of society in a democratic direction,' and (c) 'support for national and economic independence' (Rudebeck, 1982, p. 157).

Thus, during the 1970s, Sweden sought to expand its foreign aid policy into one that was internationally oriented. The work was to be characterized by the following general goals, according to Ernect Michanek:

1. To awaken and guide public opinion and gradually make the Swedish people aware of the world they live in and the global society that was emerging.

2. To give domestic decision-makers a more active role in international policy-making and strengthen the agencies within Sweden and on the International level that formulate international policy.

3. To put the people of the developing countries in the center of development co-operation programs.

4. To design Sweden's policy towards developing countries and Sweden's participation in the UN so that Swedes can systematically support, strengthen and complement international efforts in the poorer countries as a whole.

5. To concentrate Sweden's resources on a few key issues and topics, and attempt to play a major role in world developments in these fields. The issue of population should receive the highest priority.

6. To expand and take full advantage of Sweden's resources, in order to place Swedish research facilities at the disposal of international development work.

7. To find ways to take advantage of the skills and resources of all those who wish to participate in development work: young people, national organizations, business corporations, etc. (Michanek, 1971, pp. 67-71).

These criteria, and especially the objectives pointed out by Rudebeck, were designed to rule out several traditional recipients of Swedish aid in the long-run. For example, imperial Ethiopia and Pakistan would become ineligible, while states such as Tanzania and Zambia would receive more aid and new ones such as the Democratic Republic of Vietnam, Chile, Cuba and the national liberation groups in Southern Africa would become eligible (Rudebeck, 1982, pp. 157-158).

The cases of the three new recipients of Swedish aid, however, deserve additional comments because of their uniqueness. Chile, for example, began receiving Swedish aid in 1970 as support for the popular-front government of President Salvador Allende. But after the military coup in 1973, which brought an end to the Chilean experiment in Democratic Socialism, Sweden decided to halt its aid to that country (Rudebeck, 1982, p. 160).

Also, as a result of the constant criticism from the non-Socialist parties in the Riksdag in connection with Fidel Castro's active military support for the threatened independent government in Angola, Swedish aid to Cuba was reduced in 1976. It was further reduced in 1978 and 1979 to $6.7 million, after having reached a peak of $16 million in 1974. And when the Swedish Conservative Party emerged victorious in the 1979 general election, the party requested a sizeable reduction in the aid to Vietnam–a response to Vietnam's invasion of Kampuchea and its refugee policies. Consequentially, the new center-right coalition government that was formed after the election was able to maneuver the Riksdag to approve the legislation that reduced the amount of aid that was to go to Vietnam and, more importantly, reduced to one-year (instead of long-term) Swedish aid agreements with that country (Rudebeck, 1982, p. 160).

What eventually occurred during the 1970s and lasted into the 1980s was that the scope of Swedish aid to Africa became quite extraordinary. As Marquis Childs pointed out, the list of Swedish aid-recipients in Africa included Angola, Botswana, Cape Verde, Ethiopia, Guinea Bissau, Lesotho, Somalia, Swaziland, Tunisia and Zambia. In addition, Sweden provided assistance to the East African Community (EAC) and other activities such as research institutions scattered all over the continent. Emphasis was placed on the independent states in Southern Africa to help them in their support of the liberation struggle in Namibia and South Africa. During this period (1970s), Tanzania came forth as the largest recipient of Swedish aid in Africa, receiving $50 million in the 1977-1978 budget alone (Childs, 1980, p. 152). The reasons for this development are discussed in Chapter 5.

In Asia, Sweden's bilateral aid was more narrowly distributed in the 1970s. Bangladesh and Laos, two countries that were in greater need, appropriately became significant beneficiaries of Swedish aid. For example, in the 1977-1978 budget, both countries received $25 million and $9 million, respectively.

India, the largest recipient of Swedish aid in Asia, received $60 million, Sri Lanka $17 million, and Pakistan $7 million during that same budget period. In addition, Swedish aid in the aggregate of $200 million went to disaster relief, special programs, humanitarian aid to Latin America and voluntary organizations. Only Cuba saw its aid budget cut from $10 million to $8 million in the 1977-1978 budget (Childs, 1980, pp. 152-153).

But what is more important about Swedish aid in the 1970s was that it was thoroughly planned. As Childs avowed,

> Commitments are made for a three-year period after extensive consultation with representatives of the recipient countries. This is in conspicuous contrast with larger powers with a far greater aid potential that too often follow a slapdash, impoverished, off-again-on-again kind of programming (Childs, 1980, p. 153).

The Swedish approach definitely differs from those of the major powers whose focus is mainly on their own short-term economic, political and social gains.

Political Issues Involving the Third World

Another important aspect in Sweden's relations with the Third World is what Nils Andrén has referred to as 'engagement' in the developing states' struggle for liberation. Such an engagement, suggested Andrén, might be either material or moral, or both, and usually took place in two different spheres: (1) in public debates and (2) in official government statements and through actual actions taken by the Swedish government and the Riksdag. He further suggested that it was obviously at that first level that the greatest activity took place. And that in later years, public opinion had become overwhelming on the issue of few white-dominated enclaves, with colonial type rule in Africa just as it was in the case of Vietnam. However, Andrén noted that, despite the intensity of the debate on such issues, little was done on that of South Africa in terms of official measures. His reasoning for such a shortcoming hinged on the fact that the debate took place largely between groups that were outside of politics proper, with limited knowledge of international affairs (Andrén, 1967, pp. 155-156).

As far as the South African situation was concerned, Andrén believed that Sweden's actions toward the problem were primarily in the direction of public statements against Apartheid and support for UN resolutions on the issue. He further contended that Sweden had for long displayed an attitude of 'dualism' toward the Pretoria regime. He described this attitude by stating the following:

Public opinion has been exposed to a sustained effort to bring home the viciousness of the Boer nationalist rule and the plight of the colored and Negro groups in South Africa. Strong and nationwide organizations have supported the South African campaign which has also enjoyed some curious support from the Government. On the other hand, Swedish firms have made profitable investments in the rapidly expanding South African economy (Andrén, 1967, p. 156).

Another Third World political issue on which Sweden took a super-power (the United States) head on was the Vietnam War. But as Andrén noted, the Vietnam issue was difficult to fit into the general Swedish policy as it relates to its (Sweden) relations with the developing states (Andrén, 1967, p. 156). An examination of Sweden's role in the Vietnam conflict, hence, becomes essential if one is to grasp the substance of Sweden's position on such a critical issue.

For Sweden, the Vietnam issue was so vital to its moral principles that it was willing to risk its cordial relations with the United States. Sweden's plight in the Vietnam conflict was concisely stated by the Minister for International Development Cooperation at the time, Gertrud Sigurdson (during her speech at Vallingby, Stockholm, on January 27, 1975), when she said:

> Throughout we have sided with the Vietnamese in their struggle. We have done this in the firm conviction that small nations must be entitled to decide their own destinies without interference from the great powers. For this reason we have found it natural to lend direct support to North Vietnam and the PRG (People's Revolutionary Government) in their work of reconstruction (Swedish Ministry of Foreign Affairs, 1978, p. 214).

Sweden's support for North Vietnam in the conflict, as to be expected, did create some friction between Sweden and the United States. As Board suggested, the Vietnam issue became one of the most unexpected turns in the history of Swedish-American relations. The controversy between the two countries began to develop in 1967-1968 when America decided to play a combative role in Vietnam. Thus, in a country which one could have anticipated pro-American sentiments in the conflict, public opinion instead became vehemently opposed to the American presence in Vietnam. This development was so strong that Swedish-American relations were strained for quite some time (Board, 1970, p. 204).

As Board further noted, the Swedish policy posture that later took hold against the United States in the Vietnam War dates back to the era after World War II. Since that War, the Swedish public and the government decided not to play a passive role on events that occur elsewhere in the world. This desire was typified by the fact that Sweden chose not to be silent on earlier international issues such as the Communist coup in Czechoslovakia, the Berlin Blockage, the North Korean invasion of South Korea, and the USSR's suppression of the Hungarian Revolt. Therefore, as stated above, Sweden sided with the liberation forces in Southern Africa and struggles against military dictatorships like the one that ensued after the coup in Greece in November 1973. There has also been considerable and frequently expressed sympathy for the struggle of African Americans in their pursuit for complete equality in the United States (Board, 1970).

Board went on to argue that such Swedish sentiments are manifestations of Swedish morality–a type of morality that plays a significant role in modern Swedish political and social life and, therefore, quite understandable. And that what many observers outside Sweden cannot understand is how Swedes have projected their morality onto international affairs, and how such a 'proclivity' can be meshed with Sweden's neutrality policy. To this query, Board noted that Swedes have been quick to point out the distinction between their discernment of neutrality vis-à-vis that of Switzerland. For the Swedes, 'neutrality should not stop you from being able to express your views. Neutrality gives us the right, if not the duty, to say what Swedish opinion might be on issues of importance' (Board, 1970, p. 204).

For the Swedes, such a position is by no means unusual. The rationale for such an 'active neutrality' is a demonstration of the belief that if a small country is to play a role in international activities other than being passive, then, the only way to make its voice heard depends on its ability for impartiality and willingness to express moral judgements on critical issues (Board, 1970, pp. 204-205).

Thus, both the Swedish government and the opposition took stands against the war in Vietnam. Sweden went as far as granting a kind of asylum to American military deserters. Small but clamorous Swedish groups engaged in a kind of guerilla warfare directed against American diplomats and symbols in Sweden. Windows of official American buildings were shattered, American flags were set ablaze, and near-riotous demonstrations took place almost everyday in the Stockholm area. These acts compelled the American Administration in early 1968 to indicate its displeasure by recalling its ambassador to Washington for prolonged consultations (Board, 1970, p. 205).

But as Board also correctly pointed out, a distinction should be made between the acts of the Swedish government and those of privately organized groups for the sake of fairness. As he stated,

Government repeatedly stated that it opposed only the war, and that it was not associating itself with other acts of anti-Americanism. Within private groups, a similar distinction could be observed. Some of the more spectacular protests were led by left-wing extremists groups (*Vansterextrenister*) inspired by a bitter and complete hostility toward the United States in general. By far the greater part of the private opposition, however, has come from moderate groups who opposed the United States not for what it was, but for what it was doing in Vietnam, and because they felt that an obsolete American foreign policy might lead to another world war (Board, 1970, p. 205).

While this review of Sweden's relations with the Third World is neither comprehensive, nor the discussion on the areas probed exhausted, it has been possible to see (in a small way, of course) how that country's (Sweden) size and neutrality policy imposed certain limitations that allowed Sweden to escape some of those limitations with which the super-powers must contend. Thus, Sweden's relations with the Third World were outgrowths of that country's economic strength and its drive for international autonomy. These desires, therefore, dictated the rules that internal political actors must abide by in shaping Swedish-Third World relations. The rules, in turn, were outcomes of different political and ideological interests within the Swedish polity.

Chapter 4

Factors that Shaped Sweden's Policy

This chapter focuses on those factors that were thought to influence Sweden's anti-apartheid policy. They include the country's economic power, polity, debate over the choice of a socio-economic strategy, relations with other Western/Capitalist States, relations with Communist/Socialist States, and relations with South Africa.

Sweden's Economic Power

Although the concept of power has long been central to the study of international relations, it still remains vague and illusive. Nonetheless, many political scientists have long since come to grips with the reality that power is inextricably linked to political actions. Hans Morgenthau, for example, posited that for states to pursue their external goals, they need resources of power, influence, or a combination of the two (1954, p.35). But even with this definition, the operationalization of the concept of power remains wanting.

Since the early 1950s , a great deal of attention has been attributed to the problems of defining and measuring power. Robert Dahl, for example, defined power as 'the ability to shift the probability of outcomes' (1957, pp. 201-205). He suggested that one way to measure power is to employ the proceedings of political bodies like the UN and examine the number of times that a political actor votes with the majority. But such a measurement will clearly fail to show the differences between leaders and those led.

Another attempt to quantify power was that of Karl Deutsch. He viewed power as a means by which its possessors can pursue their goals. Deutsch suggested three dimensions of power that can be measured: (1) domain (internal and external), (2) range, and (3) scope (Deutsch, 1968, pp. 21-39). Attempts to operationalize these dimensions will present formidable obstacles. For instance, how can one measure external domain when it is so difficult to even quantify and rank certain states according to their abilities to use power beyond their borders.

Also, A. F. K. Organski identified six determinants of power: (1) population, (2) political development, (3) economic development, (4) national moral, (5) resources, and (6) geography. But admitting the fact that it is impracticable to use all six of these determinants, Organski suggested that GNP (GDP for this study) or GNP/GDP per capita constitutes perhaps the best index of a particular state's power (1958, p. 207).

Quite appropriately, in order to effectively pursue its foreign aid policy, Olav Stokke (1978) noted that Sweden had for many years set its total aid expenditure at one percent of its annual GDP. Sweden's GDP rose rapidly in the early 1960s, rose moderately from 1965 to 1980, declined slightly from 1981 through 1983, and then rose again in 1984. Unlike the early 1960s, the conditions for the growth of the Swedish economy during the 1965-1970 period centered on the 'diminishing supply of labor, stronger fluctuations in international business activity and a deficit on the balance of current payments' (Swedish Ministry of Finance, 1971, p. 10). But from the early 1970s to the mid-1980s, the Swedish economy experienced imbalances. Like many other industrialized countries which experienced economic setbacks during that period, Sweden also encountered weaker growth that was accompanied by increased inflation. Many factors were responsible for this outcome. The most important ones included the increases in the prices of oil and raw materials during the 1970s. These increases occurred in conjunction with the final phase of two economic upswings appropriately referred to as OPEC-I (1973-1974) and OPEC-II (1979-1980). The price increases helped to stymie the stabilization policies of the industrialized countries. And because of the deterioration of trade relations that followed the price increases, Sweden had to face the increases with a strong inflationary impulse and increased deficit on current account (Swedish Ministry of Economic Affairs, 198, p. 21).

As to be expected, the effect on the terms of trade also gave rise to falling real income that helped to lower effective demand and reduce employment. Because of this interplay, Sweden decided to adopt an expansive line in an attempt to bridge the recession during the time of OPEC-I. Meanwhile, other industrialized states opted for relatively restrictive policies (Swedish Ministry of Economic Affairs, 1982, p. 21). Quite clearly, the Swedish strategy during the time of OPEC-I was bent on protecting its position in the world market. But the attendant effect to such a strategy was usually the flooding of the market with goods and services that limited the 'opportunity' or carrying capacity for the competing countries to use the market (a theoretical discussion of this phenomenon is presented in a latter section of this chapter).

Moreover, what was even more dramatic is the fact that the shift in relative energy prices that resulted because of the increased need for oil also necessitated structural changes in the production and utilization of energy. This was due to the fact that the production apparatus and capital stock of the industrialized states in the early 1970s were tailored for the prevailing prices of energy and oil in the 1960s. Furthermore, in order to adjust to the new prices at full capacity utilization, massive new investments and the move toward production of new goods for the market were imperative. However, the industrialized economies were not sufficiently flexible enough to embark upon such ventures. Thus, the inflexibility of these economies contributed to the depressed economic conditions created by the increases in oil prices (Swedish Ministry of Economic Affairs, 1982, p. 21).

In addition, the rapid industrialization that took place in some of the developing countries accentuated the need for adjustment and change in the industrialized states. Thus, for goods that carried lower prices, the newly industrializing countries were able to displace the corresponding activities in the traditional industrialized states (Swedish Ministry of Economic Affairs, 1982, p. 22). This development certainly perpetuated some structural problems in some sectors of the industrialized economies. Sweden, for example, saw its steel industry become virtually obsolete. Such an interplay became the recipe for the new protectionism that was witnessed in the industrialized economies.

Another factor was that of low growth of productivity in the industrialized economies during the seventies. Indeed, many economic indicators pointed to the fact that poorer productivity in these economies hinged on the changes in the early part of the seventies. This view was supported by the fact that for most countries, including Sweden, the break in the productivity could be traced back to 1973 (McLaughlin, 1979). In 1973, there was a fourfold jump in oil prices, and the economic recession it partially caused dramatized the strong link between the cost of energy and the economic growth in all countries (for more details, the interested reader can consult McLaughlin, 1979). Moreover, the low capacity utilization which proved to be in paramount reason for the poor development of productivity in the 1970s was possible because of the inability of Sweden to undertake the structural changes dictated by the new relative prices (Swedish Ministry of Economic Affairs, 1982, p. 22).

Because of that, the lower growth rate of productivity was not accompanied by a corresponding adjustment of minimal earnings and unit costs, therefore, went up. With these costs came higher rates of inflation. And with the higher inflation rates came slightly higher rates of unemployment in the seventies (Swedish Ministry of Economic Affairs, 1982, p. 22). These developments, thus, brought with them inevitable political changes in the industrialized states. For example, in Sweden, Olof Palme was once again elected to the Riksdag on his promise to create new jobs and reduce the inflation rate. And in France, a Socialist government was formed and headed by President François Mitterrand on the same promise.

Partly because inflation remained high even when the price increases for oil had been absorbed, and partly because of the ups and downs of the financial markets, the recovery that could have been realized after OPEC-I never materialized. During this same period, interest and exchange rates in the industrialized economies increased sharply. And when the inflation rates began to decline, the expected economic upswing was deterred because real interest remained high. The attendant developments in the United States also played an important role during this period. The conflict in America between a tight, consistent monetary policy and an increasingly large federal deficit was also to become a central thorn for economic policy (Swedish Ministry of Economic Affairs, 1982, p. 22).

This conflict between monetary policy and the federal deficit was heightened by the budget presented by the Reagan Administration in 1981 (Swedish Ministry of Economic Affairs, 1982, p. 23). This interplay prevented interest rates from falling to normal levels, an effect that was felt by Sweden and other countries (simply because the world revolved around the United States dollar).

While indicators such as stocks, profits and investments pointed to a direction for a recovery of activity in the industrialized world, these factors were counteracted by the turbulence of the financial side. High interest rates held back consumption and investments in stocks (Swedish Ministry of Economic Affairs, 1982, p. 23). Another factor that impeded the economic recovery was the difficulties encountered by Eastern European states after the wake of the 'Polish crisis.' Strikes in Gdansk and the other Baltic ports in the Summer of 1980 helped to give birth to an independent trade union named Solidarnosč (Solidarity), an unprecedented trade development in the Eastern bloc. On October 8, 1982, the Polish Parliament abolished the previously suspended independent trade union. A trade embargo by the West on Poland because of the ban created payment difficulties that subscribed to what is known as the 'Polish Crisis' (*The Economist* 16-22 October, 1982, vol. 285, no. 7259, p. 67; *International Herald Tribune,* Monday, March 28, 1983, no. 3, 133, p. 1). This also meant that the West was discouraged from supplying credit to the eastern European states, thereby creating depressive effects on both the East and the West (Swedish Ministry of Economic Affairs, 1982, p. 23).

Thus, because of the fact that Sweden's annual foreign aid to the developing countries equaled one percent of its annual GDP, Sweden's economic history dictated the actual amount of aid that went to the front-line states and the Southern African liberation forces. Hence, the aid increased during those years when the Swedish economy grew (Bangura, 1987, p. 116). How does Sweden's economic policy fit in all this?

The most important objective of Sweden's economic policy is the maintenance of full employment. This preoccupation, which also helped Sweden to achieve high GDP rates over the years, was spurred by circumstances that prevailed in the country during World Wars I and II. The average unemployment rate during this period was 15 per cent. Between 1923 and 1930, the average unemployment rate was 11 per cent; from 1930 to 1933, the average rate climbed up to 19 percent; during the 1933-1937 period, it declined slightly to 16 per cent; and from 1937 to 1939, the average unemployment rate stood at the 16 per cent mark (Schnitzer, 1967, p. 8).

After World War II, however, Sweden, for many years, was able to maintain an average unemployment rate of less than two per cent. As a matter of fact, the shortage of labor supply in some parts of the country compelled employers to bring in workers from other countries (Schnitzer, 1967, pp. 8-9).

The reason for Sweden's economic success can be traced to the fact that its neutralist policy kept the Swedes from the two World Wars that brought destruction to the economies of other European states. However, in order for the Swedish government to pursue its policy of high employment in the post-war period, it meant that monetary and fiscal policies had to take a back seat in the process. As Martin Schnitzer observed,

> Throughout most of the post war period, the Swedish economy has labored under inflationary pressures as the government has pursued a cheap money policy as an integral part of its full employment and social welfare program. When a general decline in economic activity occurs, a series of employment measures are used, including emergency public works, extra government orders from industry, and accelerated building construction (Schnitzer, 1967, p. 9).

Thus, Sweden's preoccupation with maintaining a high level of employment, with the attendant high GDP, also meant continued trade and diplomatic relations with South Africa. As pointed out earlier, the Swedish government believed that discontinuing such relations, no matter its feelings about Apartheid, would mean the loss of jobs for those Swedes who worked for companies that did business either in or with South Africa.

The Nature of Sweden's Polity

The foreign policy of any state is the outcome of both internal and external inputs. It is also important to note that there is not a single foreign policy-making process in any given state, but many policy-making processes that vary from issue to issue. It is, therefore, appropriate to posit that the nature of a given state's polity determines the type of foreign policy-making process that is employed on a particular issue.

As R. Barry Farrell aptly suggested, there exist certain relationships between internal political settings and international politics for some states. And these relationships vary for 'open' and 'closed' political systems. Farrell went on to assert the following:

> The term "open political system" will be used as synonymous with constitutional democracy. And its characteristics are competitive regular electoral contests, legalized two or multi-party organizations aimed at offering alternative governmental leadership, a high degree of toleration for autonomous groups in politics, and an acceptance of constitutional restraints on governmental power. Closed systems will be thought of as coming under a totalitarian model...an official ideology, a single mass party constituting a relatively small percentage of the total population, a system of terroristic police control, near-complete party control of all means of effective mass communication (Farrell, 1971, p. 88).

From these definitions, Sweden can be regarded as an 'open' society. The openness of the society is typified by facts such as picking up a telephone directory in Stockholm and seeing the profession of each person listed in it. I was even surprised by the fact that my course grades were publicly displayed at Stockholms Universitet for all those interested to see them. It is the spirit of such openness that has made Sweden one of the stronger democracies in the world. And its parliamentary system has facilitated the continued openness of the society.

Furthermore, the *Instrument of Government* enacted in 1974 rests in the hands of Swedish people all political powers. This Act stipulates that popular sovereignty should be based on the principles of 'universal' and 'equal' suffrage' within the framework of 'representative government' (Wadensjö, 1979, p. 87). And since about 90 per cent of the Swedish voters do cast their votes on any given election, this strengthens the stability of this truly 'representative democracy.'

In order to obtain a distribution of seats in the parliament that is equitable to all political parties in Sweden, a minimum criterion was set for the allocation of the seats: a party is entitled some seats if it wins at least four per cent of the total number of votes cast in an election nationwide; a party that wins at least 12 per cent of the total votes cast in a particular constituency gets some seats within that country, even though it may fail to fulfill the four per cent criterion (Wadensjö, 1979, p. 87). This means that any party that wins the most number of seats in the 310 constituencies to form a majority in parliament stands a better chance of dominating the Swedish foreign policy-making arena.

This was the norm until 1976 when Swedish governments commanded a majority in parliament. The Social Democratic Party, in particular, has always presented strong governments that dominated the Swedish political arena for approximately seven decades. When in need of a coalition, the Social Democrats would always align themselves with socialist parties because they all belong to the ideological left. However, the non-socialist parties were able to form a coalition government after the 1976 election. After a few years of Liberal Party government, the non-socialist parties were once again able to gain control of the government with a one-seat majority in the 1979 election (Wadensjö, 1979, pp. 84-85). The Social Democratic Party, under the leadership of Olof Palme, took control of the government after the 1982 elections.

Quite obviously, since the elected government exercises executive power, presents new legislation, proposes budgets, issues statutes and maintains the country's international relations, it can be asserted that the number of seats a particular party has in parliament will dictate its position in Sweden's foreign policy-making processes. Thus, what made Sweden's liberation support possible may be explained by the legacy that the Social Democratic Party had created in the Swedish society. As Francis Castle suggested, the non-socialist political parties operated within the framework of similar sets of beliefs about welfare and equality as does the Social Democratic Party. Castle arrived at this conclusion after examining the actions used by the various Swedish political parties on achieving office that showed 'indirect evidence for the bourgeois parties' adherence to the social democratic image of society' (Castle, 1977, pp. 7-10). Thus, whether in decline or in strength, the Social Democrats' position on liberation support was never affected. However, it is not enough to simply state this maxim if one is to understand why Sweden's political parties share certain political attitudes akin to the egalitarian welfare orientation. A further probing of the country's political system is, therefore, in order.

A survey of the literature on the Swedish political system makes it possible to delineate two key approaches on the subject: (1) the Group Approach (Pluralism and Neo-corporatism)–those who see the Swedish political system as one that operates in a democratic industrialized society and, therefore, serves as an arena for compatibility and conflict between interest groups; and (2) the Class Approach–those who descry the Swedish political system as one dominated by three big class parties. Their sources of analysis are usually, if not exclusively, drawn from election results and studies of the society. Given these two categories, the following model is generated into which the studied literature on Sweden's political system can sensibly be placed (see Table 4.1). Noting that the model is not exhaustive, a discussion on the two categories is called for.

The Group Approach (Pluralism and Neo-corporatism)

First of all, an explanation for why scholars using the concepts 'pluralism' and 'neo-corporatism' should be considered scholars of the group approach is useful at this juncture. According to Victor Pestoff, these scholars view popular movements and interest organizations as *groups* comprising of a social sub-system within the larger political system. Thus, any strain or conflict that takes place within that sub-system will also be felt in the political system at large. Democratic processes at the macro-level are, therefore, affected and, in turn, affect popular movements and interest organizations. The general questions that arise from these scholars, hence, include: (a) How can citizens structure the relationship between the state and themselves on the one hand, and interest organizations and other non-governmental organizations on the other hand in democratic societies? (b) What tasks should the organizations perform as far as the state and the citizens are concerned one at a time as part of an overall democratic society? (Pestoff, 1982, p.1). Now, separate discussions on the two concepts are necessary.

Pluralism

The most widely used hypothesis in pluralist literature is that which focuses on multiple memberships and cross-pressures. According to this hypothesis, citizens in modern democratic societies are members of several groups. And because most of these citizens also maintain overlapping memberships in these groups, it leads to cross-pressures at various levels in society such as the political system. These cross-pressures are, therefore, considered beneficial for the maintenance and stability of the political system (Pestoff, 1982, p. 3).

However, Pestoff has found that the pluralist model fared little better when put under an empirical test. For example, in Sweden, Pestoff (1982, p. 4) found slightly less than half of the adults maintained multiple memberships in organizations. This limitation led P. C. Schmitter to champion an alternative research strategy that has assumed the concept of neo-corporatism.

Table 4.1 Approaches on the Swedish Political System

The Group Approach (Pluralism and Neo-corporatism)	The Class Approach
Back, 1976	Anton, 1980
Dallenbrant and Pestoff, 1980	Berglung and Lindstrom, 1978
Ekerberg, 1981	Inglehart, 1977
Huntford, 1972	Koblik, 1975
Korpi, 1979	Lewin, 1972
Lembruch, 1977	Pettersson, 1978
Pestoff, 1970 and 1977	Scase, 1977
Ruin, 1974	Särlvik, 1974 & 1977
Schmitter, 1974 and 1981	Tomasson, 1970
Solvang and Moren, 1974	

Neo-Corporatism

Scholars who employ this concept make variations between 'societal corporatism' and 'state corporatism.' They treat the former as something imposed as part of a 'grand design' to structure society in such a way as to eradicate conflicts between various social groups. And they treat the latter as something imposed by the state, such as Benito Mussolini's attempts to eliminate those associations that united Italian employers and employees. The societal variant, which encourages the functions of interest organizations to intermediate between the state and its citizens, is, therefore, referred to as neo-corporatism (Pestoff, 1982, p. 4-5).

And as Solvang and Moren have shown, certain interest groups have been able to have continued access to the Swedish administrative level of government because of their abundant organizational resources, while others gain access only as the political conditions avail themselves. For example, they pointed out the fact that Swedish landlords, commercial and business groups had been able to influence decision-making at the administrative level of government because of the great amount of organizational resources at their disposal (Solvang and Moren, 1974, pp. 32-50).

However, the Swedish government had long since entered the business of financing interest organizations that lack the necessary resources to be able to generate organizational tools in order to get their voices heard in the society. As Pestoff pointed out, more than 1.5 billion crowns were granted by the Riksdag to organizations as direct financial support in the 1976-1977 budget. In the 1977-1978 budget, nearly two billion crowns were appropriated for the organizations. Also, the Ministry of Education contributed three-fifths, the Ministry of Labor about one-eighth, and the Ministry of Agriculture gave seven percent of the total direct financial support to Swedish organizations (Pestoff, 1982, p. 13). In spite of all this, there are other scholars who look at the Swedish political system as one that operates in a capitalist society and, therefore, open to social class competition. These scholars can be said to employ the class approach.

The Class Approach

For authors using the class approach to investigate the Swedish political system, it is dominated by three big class parties: the Social Democrat, the Agrarian, and the Conservative. These scholars look at the electoral bases of these parties in order to explain class voting and to find similar patterns of social factors that influence class voting. They also examine the psychological variables that influence the Swedish voter, possible decline in class voting, and the distinctness of the Swedish party system compared to other types.

Thus, Berglund and Lindstrom (1978) have explained the dominance of the Social Democratic Party in the Swedish political system as a result of the party's typical class base. According to these authors, the Social Democrats emerged because the lower class wanted to exploit its numerical strength as its main political resource, and which it felt was ignored by the existing political parties. They maintain that the conditions were favorable for the creation of the Social Democratic Party for the lower class: type of income, working conditions, social status and educational background. Thus, the Social Democrats became closely associated with the trade union movement and those organizations that sought the interests of the working class such cooperatives, housing societies, sick-benefit associations and adult education societies. Berglund and Lindstrom, however, cautioned that, even though the Social Democratic Party is a class party, not all workers cast their votes in its favor. While some workers prefer the bourgeois parties, others vote for other left-wing parties. Nonetheless, class analysts over the years have become increasingly aware of the certainty that changes are taking place in the class party system, although the degrees to these changes and their perceived outcomes may vary from scholar to scholar.

Bo Särlvik (1977, pp. 73-129), for example, suggested that the stability of Swedish voting behavior had given way to a greater mobility, and that the stable balance of strength between the parties had been disturbed during recent elections. He noted that traditional parties had to change their styles and images in their efforts to attract new members outside their original social core. A good example is that the Swedish Center Party, which from a mere nine percent of the vote in 1956 received 24 per cent of the vote in 1976. Furthermore, Särlvik pointed out the facts that contemporary issues tended to favor some parties over others, and it had become easier for new parties to break into the political arena.

Given this backdrop, the contention that non-socialist parties operated within the framework of similar sets of beliefs about welfare and equality as did the Social Democrats carries a lot of weight. Thus, whether in decline or in strength, the Social Democrats' position, which saw the Apartheid issue as one of equity, was never contorted by the other political parties in Sweden. Indeed, this was a significant outcome of the nature of the Swedish political system.

Debate Over the Choice of a Socio-economic Strategy

Acknowledging the fact that Sweden was caught in a 'technology and socio-economic trap,' two major approaches were suggested to free Sweden from those 'traps': (1) further technological innovation suggested by the Organization for Economic Cooperation and Development (OECD) and (2) further state intervention suggested by the Swedish Labor Union (LO) in its call for a Wage-earners' Fund. But before discussing these proposals, it makes sense to explore some questions about Sweden's position in the international socio-economic arena that sparked the debate.

What were the underlying reasons for the continued economic and social problems in the industrial economy of Sweden? What were the perceived consequences of these problems upon the domestic politics and the international relations of Sweden? What domestic and foreign policies were suggested for Sweden to pursue to bring about a return to sustained economic prosperity? These were troubling questions for Sweden at the time, as all indicators pointed to the fact that the country was caught up in what Denis Pirages (1978, pp. 186-188) once called the 'technology and socio-economic trap.'

What does this 'trap' mean? Citing biologist Garret Hardin's metaphor that aptly described one of the impacts of technology on relations among nations,

Pirages pointed out that Hardin's image is one of tragedies that unfolded on a medieval 'commons'–an area open to all herdsmen to pasture their livestock. The tragedy that develops on the commons is related to the fact that there is only limited 'opportunity' or carrying capacity for herdsmen to use it. In the absence of accepted institutionalized regulations governing the use of the commons, each herdsman will attempt to put as many animals as possible on it because it seems to be in his self-interest to do so. Within the industrial paradigm of capitalist societies, which emphasizes minimal government interference in economic matters, there is great resistance to rules limiting individual initiatives in using such commons. Given a limited commons and increased participants, a tragedy unfolds as the commons is decimated by excessive grazing. The herds on it collapse due to starvation. Each individual actor is locked into a system that encourages the relatively unbridled pursuit of self-interest on a free, but finite, commons. Within the ethical system that is at the core of the expansionist industrial paradigm, freedom on a commons, thus, brings ruin to all (Pirages, 1978, p. 186).

Pirages noted that the tragedy of the commons is rooted in the fact that human beings are ill-equipped psychologically to link their short-term actions with long-term consequences. In some cases, this instability is simply due to individual selfishness. In the absence of strong ethical principles to the contrary, selfish individuals on the commons may not care that it will ultimately collapse because they may have plans to market their herds early and invest the proceeds in other pursuits. In other cases, such apparently shortsighted behavior may be due to lack of appropriate information. Each herdsman may not realize that others are acting similarly or that the commons has limited capacity. There are still others who are willingly ignorant of the future impact of their actions. Advocates of this 'eat, drink, and be merry' philosophy may not care that there would not be a common left for those generations yet to come (Pirages, 1978, p. 186).

The tragedy of the commons, emphasized Pirages, is one variation of a larger set of dilemmas that could be called problems of coordination. If the world were a perfectly rational place run by perfectly rational individuals possessing perfect information, tragedies of this nature would not take place. Appropriate ethics and laws would govern the use of such commons in the interest of the welfare of present and future generations. Unfortunately, when confronting these issues the world is far from being rational at present. In international affairs, there are no commonly accepted policies governing commons in the interest of all humanity. Even if there were such policies, it is very unlikely that the actions of individual 'sovereign' countries could be coordinated to bring about a desired future. Each nation in the international system usually attempts to maximize its own self-interest, disregarding the common interest of all others (Pirages, 1978, pp. 186-187).

Citing Robert Godding, Pirages defined a coordination problem as one existing whenever it is rational for all agents involved to prefer joint to independent decision making. There are two necessary conditions for the existence of a coordination problem: (1) actors must be mutually involved, and (2) there must be danger of disagreeable outcomes for everyone if all individuals act independently. In the case of Hardin's commons, Pirages noted that the tragedy unfolds because all actors are mutually dependent upon one piece of real estate and do not act accordingly or collectively to avert the collapse of the herds. In international relations, it is becoming the more obvious that the delicate nature of the ecosystem and the relatively limited quantities of some critical natural resources make all nations much more mutually dependent. And if nations continue to act in their perceived short-run self-interest in these matters, as they have throughout most of the Industrial Revolution, their actions will lead to a disagreeable outcome for the collective (Pirages, 1978, p.187). This analogy is akin to Sweden's role in international socio-economic activities from the 1970s to the 1980s.

John Platt used the term 'social-traps' to refer to situations where individual actors, organizations, or whole societies get themselves involved in a course of action or set of relationships that later prove to be unpleasant or lethal. He analyzed a series of situations in which all actors collectively suffer because of individuals who act in what they perceive to be their self-interest while the situation changes. The essence of such traps, therefore, is that the self-interested behavior that gathers momentum in one set of circumstances cannot be rapidly changed to conform to a new set of circumstances (Pirages, 1978, p. 187). The terminology, 'social-traps,' is, thus, apt to the international socio-economic activities that ensued from the 1970s to the 1980s.

When dominant social paradigms are in transition, the number of social, political and economic traps in which people see themselves tend to increase rapidly. Tragedies of the commons, problems of coordination, and social traps are, therefore, many in the global political economy. A majority of them can be said to have been precipitated by the rapid and unequal growth of technology. The most obvious category of such socio-economic problems is parallel to Hardin's medieval tragedy and is based upon 'cutthroat' competition among individual nations for limited natural resources. Technological development and industrial growth have created an international social trap in energy markets. The industrialized countries remain locked in a growth paradigm that makes them increasingly vulnerable to the machinations of less developed petroleum exporters (Pirages, 1978, pp. 187-188), despite the temporary strains they are facing right now. To escape this vulnerability, industrialized countries have tried to develop alternative fuels, some of which have created many environmental threats including nuclear reactor accidents (notably, Three Mile Island) and through military control (e.g., the United States' invasion and occupation of Iraq). The only ethical way out of this trap is to rethink the core assumption inherent in the growth paradigm.

Sweden in the International Socio-economy (1970s-1980s)

The findings of a quantitative study done by the Swedish Ministry of Economic Affairs provided a picture of Sweden's socio-economic posture in the global arena from the 1970s through the 1980s. The study acknowledged that Sweden was beset, along with most industrialized countries, by a profound lack of economic balance and that restoring equilibrium would require substantial structural changes in the economy that would take several years to achieve (Swedish Ministry of Economic Affairs, 1982, p. 19).

It was maintained that the imbalances in the Swedish economy at the time were the result of developments in the 1970s. Along with many other industrialized states which had experienced economic setbacks during that decade, Sweden was also experiencing a weaker growth accompanied by increased unemployment and inflation. There were many reasons for this dilemma. One of the major reasons was the price increases for oil and raw materials during the 70s. These increases occurred in conjunction with the final phase of two economic upswings which were referred to as OPEC-I (1973-1974) and OPEC-II (1979-1980). These price increases aided to 'throttle' the upswings and managed to meet the stabilization policy of the industrialized states with quite a dilemma (Swedish Ministry of Economic Affairs, 1982, p. 21). Sweden and other non-OPEC countries had to face the price increases with a strong 'inflationary impulse' and increased 'deficit on current account' due to the deterioration of trade relations that accompanied the price increases.

It should be noted that the effect on terms of trade also gives rise to falling real income, which in turn helps to lower effective demand, and thereby tends to reduce employment. Thus, because of the stabilization policy, the industrialized countries were now faced with a choice between combating price increases and the deficit on current account by means of restrictive fiscal and monetary policies for the short run, with the attendant risk of inflation running wild. In lieu of this interplay, Sweden and some countries followed the OECD recommendation at the time to bridge the recession while other countries chose a relatively restrictive policy (Swedish Ministry of Economic

Affairs, 1982, p. 21). Sweden's policy at the time was reminiscent of the analogy of the commons, especially when the tragedy developed because of the limited 'opportunity' or carrying capacity for the industrialized countries to use the global market. It is, therefore, safe to state that it was 'unwise' for Sweden to have embarked upon an expansive line as recommended by the OECD at the time of OPEC-I, because it jeopardized the chances of those countries which depended on the market for their basic survival.

However, it was maintained that the shift in relative energy as a result of the increases for oil also necessitated structural changes in the production apparatus, and the capital stocks of the industrialized counties at the beginning of the 1970s were tailored to the relative prices of oil and energy in the 1960s. It was further suggested that an adjustment to the new prices at full capacity utilization would have required massive new investments and a switch to new production processes. This was the kind of development which many economists foresaw at the time of OPEC-I. However, the industrialized economies did not prove sufficiently flexible, at least in practice. The necessary adjustment had also been impeded by the depressive economic climate which the price increases for oil had contributed to create (Swedish Ministry of Economic Affairs, 1982, p. 21).

The need for adjustment and change in industrialized countries was accentuated by the rapid pace of industrialization that was taking place in some developing countries. It was, therefore, assumed that by means of lower prices, those newly industrializing state could have knocked out corresponding activities in the traditional industrialized countries (Swedish Ministry of Economic Affairs, 1982, p. 22). It is, thus, safe to suggest that this interplay fostered certain structural dilemmas in the 'traditional industrialized countries,' with some sectors of the economies making very little profit. For example, in Sweden, the steel industry had become virtually out of existence. With these problems, one began to see a rebirth of 'protectionism' and 'subsidies' to protect certain sectors of the economy from international competition. One also began to see suspended or at least postponed adjustment that should have been made to avert new prices and the effects from the 'rugged' competition that ensued.

Another important feature was that of the low growth of productivity in the industrialized countries for the 1970s. What was also clear was how difficult it was to tell whether the extent of this slow-down of growth of productivity reflected a change in the underlying development of productivity and capacity, rather than an inability to utilize the potential growth. Whatever the response might have been, there were numerous indications that the poorer productivity was closely tied up with changes in the world economy in the early part of the

70s. This view was supported by the fact that for most countries, the break in productivity could be traced back to 1973. During this year, there was a fourfold jump in oil prices, and the economic recession it partially caused dramatized the strong links between the cost of energy and economic growth in all countries (McLaughlin, 1979). Moreover, low capacity utilization which was the paramount reason for the poor development of productivity in the 1970s was seen to have been an inability to undertake the structural changes which the relative prices dictated (Swedish Ministry of Economic Affairs, 1982, p. 22).

It was, therefore, maintained that as the lower growth of productivity had not been accompanied by the corresponding adjustment of nominal earnings, unit costs had to be boosted. And with them came the underlying rate of inflation. The structural problems in the industrialized countries helped to increase those set of problems that faced the stabilization policy. Most importantly, unemployment and inflation also increased dramatically in the 1970s (Swedish Ministry of Economic Affairs, 1982, p. 22) and set the stage for many political changes in the industrialized states. For example, in France, a Socialist government was formed headed by François-Maurice Mitterand. In Sweden, Olof Palme was once again elected to the Riksdag on his promise to create jobs and reduce inflation.

In certain respects, the adjustment by the industrialized countries to OPEC-II went a lot better compared to that of OPEC-I. One example was the impact of increased oil prices on real earnings which had been accepted relatively quickly. This meant that the 'kick' to inflation of the 1979-1980 period was smaller than that of 1973-1974. Another example was that the effect on profit margins was less marked on the second occasion—that is, 1979-1980 (Swedish Ministry of Economic Affairs, 1982, p. 22).

Any recovery which could have been realized after OPEC-I was stymied partly because inflation remained high even when the price increases for oil had been absorbed and partly because of the marked turbulence on financial markets. During the same period, interest and exchange rates in the large economies both fluctuated sharply. When rates of inflation began to decline, real interests remained very high for quite a long time, which interfered with an economic upswing. It should also be noted that developments in the United States had been particularly important during this period. The conflict in the United States between a tight, consistent monetary policy and an increasingly large federal deficit became a central problem for economic policy. The assumption that the American government's large borrowing requirement tended to push up the real interest rate was greatly supported (Swedish Ministry of Economic Affairs, 1982, p. 22). This was undoubtedly a purposefully designed policy by America to protect its hold on international economic competition.

It was also the case that the conflict between monetary policy and the federal deficit had been heightened by the budget which the Ronald Reagan Administration presented. Even if the GDP growth is looked at optimistically, it seems likely that the federal deficit did remain very large. This sustained inflationary expectations in the United States, despite the fact that the rate of inflation seemed to have been falling at the time (Swedish Ministry of Economic Affairs, 1982, pp. 22-23). It could, therefore, be suggested that the prospect of resurgent inflation and a large federal borrowing requirement tended to prevent interest rates from falling to normal levels. Such an interplay had a spreading effect on other industrialized countries, especially when 'the world revolved on the American dollar.'

There existed an indication for a recovery of activity in the industrialized countries when one looks at 'real' factors. Notably, stocks, profits and investments had been pointing in that direction. However, these factors were being counteracted by problems on the financial side. High interest rates were holding back private consumption as well as investments and stocks. Real interests would have had to come down for the industrialized countries to see an upswing. The development of interest rates was, however, highly uncertain and made the picture for socio-economic recovery blurry for the immediate outlook on international activity (Swedish Ministry of Economic Affairs, 1982, p. 23). The political tension which mounted because of the very high levels of unemployment in the industrialized countries was not at all helping any prospects for recovery.

Another factor was the payment difficulties which countries in Eastern Europe were experiencing in connection with the 'Polish crisis.' For instance, strikes in Gdansk, Poland and other Baltic ports in the summer of 1980 helped to give birth to an independent trade union named Solidarnosč (Solidarity), an unprecedented development in the Eastern bloc. On October 8, 1982, the Polish parliament abolished the previously 'suspended' independent trade union. A trade embargo by the West on Poland created payment difficulties that contributed to what came to be labeled the 'Polish crisis' (for details, see *The Economist*, October 16-22, 1982, vol. 285, no. 7259, p. 67; the *International Herald Tribune*, Monday, March 28, 1983, no. 31, 133, p. 1). This also meant that the West was discouraged from supplying credit to Poland which, in turn, caused depressive effects on both the East and the West (Swedish Ministry of Economic Affairs, 1982, p. 23).

As stated earlier, in order for Sweden to break loose from these socio-economic traps, two major propositions were debated. I shall now examine both the OECD and LO suggestions in the following two sections.

The OECD Suggestion

The 1980 OECD report stated categorically that technical innovation was absolutely central to the solution of Sweden's socio-economic difficulties. The implications of the organization's analysis were as follows:

1. It seems to us that effective demand management policies, while necessary, are not sufficient to solve the present difficulties. In particular, a number of structural problems prevent governments from using traditional methods effectively;

2. Technical innovation, far from being peripheral, is central to the solution of these problems (i.e. socio-economic traps) and can facilitate the use of demand management policies;

3. Technical advancement cannot be taken for granted. Neither the rate nor the direction can now be regarded as satisfactory. The rate has slowed down substantially, and as we shall attempt to show, the direction has meant that it is lacking in some areas where it is vitally needed;

4. While it is true that technical innovation depends to a considerable degree upon private initiative, governmental policies have an essential part to play. Among other things, such policies set the context and provide the incentive or constraints for private initiative;

5. Experience of the past quarter century shows that although some of these policies have been successful (for example, in agriculture or fundamental research), others have been inefficient or expensive (as for example, subsidizing of certain technological ventures without reference to market considerations or society's needs);

6. It is imperative not only to discriminate between good and bad policies of the past but to devise new innovation policies for the present and future; and

7. In any case, research and innovation policies must be better integrated

with other aspects of governmental policy, particularly with economic and social ones (OECD, 1980, p. 15).

The OECD report also noted that the reason for the slowdown in economic growth for the OECD countries, of which Sweden is a part, was that science and technology policies had usually been defined and implemented independently of economic policies (OECD, 1980, 12). The report further noted that there were now several 'motors' of the world economy which can be explained in part by the fact that Western Europe and Japan had recovered the economic and industrial position which they had lost because of World War II. Moreover, the recovery meant that the United States had to share the 'motor' with other OECD countries (OECD, 1980, p. 20). Not only did American have to share the 'motor' with other OECD countries, it also had to fight for its own economic survival in the international market. Indeed, this development typified Pirages' thesis on the tragedy of the common.

As Giarini and Loubergé (1978, p. 47) argued, in a given historical context, the embodiment of technical advancement in the production sphere has contributed to high growth. However, they also noted that the impact of this new factor has declined gradually. They further pointed out that the global marginal productivity of any investment in Research and Development (R and D) tended toward zero, which explained the slowdown and stoppage of growth.

Even though they accepted the fact that economic growth in the modern era was made possible by the process of technology, Giarini and Loubergé (1978, p. 44) noted that progress was not constant during the period considered. They also pointed out that growth could only be maintained and broadened because of two waves of technological discoveries. These discoveries, they stated, spread gradually through the whole economy but also caused profound structural changes while doing so. The first wave started in England in the mid-18th Century and had its initial impact on the textile industry before affecting metallurgy and transport and then dying out at the end of the 19th Century after having spread to Continental Europe and North America. The second wave, which was characterized by the union of technology and science, took shape by the end of the 19th Century and has lasted to the present and affected the whole world.

In addition, Giarini and Loubergé (1978, pp. 44-45) maintained that in many ways, the period through which Western society was passing in the 1970s might be compared with the end of the 19th Century. At that time, the economic future looked bleak and this was reflected in the return to protectionism and persistent deflation. The antagonisms that developed with the relative decline of Britain prefigured those other nations that emerged with the weakening of American leadership. Yet, it was, in fact, only a relatively brief period of transition between the era of the Industrial Revolution and that of the second. They added that this was not strictly speaking a third Industrial Revolution, but it was rather a 'second wind' of the preceding one. The linkage between science and technology was simply being reinforced; and this, in the minds of the upholders of this view of the future, was enough to prolong past economic growth.

Sigurdson (1981, p. 117), in examining the relationship between technological change and employment, with special attention to the engineering industry in Sweden, noted that initially many observers predicted that large scale introduction of microelectronics would drastically reduce employment first in the manufacturing and then in many, if not most, service sectors, with far reaching consequences for the economic sector all over the world. He further stated that these fears had been exaggerated, but that electronic technology and eventually the electronic revolution would affect all countries and influence practically every sector of the economy. However, he recognized the fact that these changes were gradual and that there were still many technological problems to be overcome. Nevertheless, the effect on enterprises or whole industrial sectors or certain categories were already very profound. What Sigurdson did not point out is that despite the fact that the electronic phase had not 'directly' reduced employment drastically, it had not created many new jobs either. Besides, it could be argued that this electronic phase indirectly helped to reduce jobs in other sectors. For example, the introduction of electronically operated gas pumps diminished the need for gas station attendants at most places.

Sigurdson (1981, p. 129) also argued that employment in industry, particularly in the engineering sector, was likely to continue to decline in the traditional sense of the industry. This indicated that the transformation of the structure of the economy in the direction of services was making up a larger share of economic activities. Given the desire for Sweden to compete with other industrially developed countries, coupled with its desire to drastically reduce its unemployment rate, it could not 'cut itself loose' from the international market. Thus, it was inevitable that the shift of employment from industry to the service sector continued in Sweden.

In relation to the gap of productivity between Japan and other industrialized countries like Sweden, Sigurdson (1981, p. 129) suggested that the other countries should have resorted to the continuous introduction of new production technology as exemplified by robots in the engineering sector.

Such a move was only bound to continue to stifle employment in the industrial sector, which the service sector would be able to manage. Moreover, Sigurdson stated the following:

> The introduction of advanced technology to increase productivity appears to have different effects. First, it replaces or rather substitutes high skilled labour as exemplified by NC-machines, which no doubts erodes the comparative advantage which the advanced industrialized countries enjoy over less developed countries. Second, the new technology, as exemplified by the robot, substitutes less skilled workers with the consequences that the advanced industrialized countries are regaining a competitive advantage. This is particularly true in sectors where research and development, production and marketing are becoming more integrated and more sophisticated and require a well developed infrastructure and highly skilled "systems operators" (Sigurdson, 1981, p. 30).

Given Sigurdson's position, an examination of the general impact of technology upon society is in order. This is essential for the mere fact that any decision made to further technological innovation in Sweden would have raised not only economic concerns but social ones as well. These concerns, in turn, would influence Sweden's policy toward South Africa.

'We dwell on the impact of the car,' asserted Robert Heilbroner, not because it is the most significant of technological changes. Before the car, there was the startling economic transformation caused by the train, and after it came the no less totally transforming effects of electrical communication.' He went on to say that 'rather, we touch on the profound economic implications of the automobile to show the diffuse effects of all industrial technology–effects which economics often cannot measure and which exceed its normal area of study but which must, nonetheless, be borne in mind as the ever-present and primary reality of the technological revolution itself' (Heilbroner, 1970, p. 92).

A review of the general effects of technology on society suggested by Heilbroner are threefold. The first general effect deals with the 'vast increase in the degree of urbanization of society.' It is maintained that to an extraordinary extent, technology has enhanced the ability of the farmer to support the non-farmer. As a result, society has more and more taken on the aspects and problems of the city rather than the countryside (Heilbroner, 1970, 92). During the last decades, population movements in Sweden had usually been in a north-south direction, from central Norland via its coastal region to the bigger towns of central and southern Sweden. In particular there had been a marked expansion of the three large urban areas in Sweden: Stockholm, Goteborge (Gothenburg), and Malmö-Lund. With the decline of its agricultural population, Sweden became an increasingly urbanized country. By 1975, 85 per cent of the population was living in towns and villages containing more than 200 inhabitants. There was also considerable movement of population within the larger towns. Town centers had been taken over by office development, banks and business premises while housing had been moved to the suburbs. It was mostly elder people who remained in the town centers while young families had to choose between renting a high-rise flat on the outskirts of the town or trying to buy a suburban villa or terraced house in one of the many residential areas that had been created, usually at a considerable distance from places of work in the town center (Wadensjö, 1979, p. 20).

The second general effect is that 'the steady growth of industrial technology has radically lessened the degree of economic independence of the average citizen.' There is the existence of extreme vulnerability of the 'unsupported' inhabitant of a modern society that is dependent on the work of a thousand others to sustain her/his existence. This has been borne out of the effect of the continuing Industrial Revolutions. Technology did not stop at taking women or men off the soil and into the city, it also vastly increased the specialized nature of work. Unlike the 'man of all trades' of the early 19th Century–the farmer who could perform so many of his necessary tasks himself, the typical factory worker or office worker is trained and employed to do only a small part of a social position which now achieves staggering complexity (Heilbroner, 1970, pp. 92-92).

In Sweden, the industrial sector which for a long time employed the largest number of people was overtaken by the service sector. The primary reason for the relative decline in industrial employment could be attributed to the increasingly rapid rate of rationalization and automation within the industrial sector. The introduction of computer technology meant that one person could now carry out a job that previously required many workers (Wadensjö, 1979, p. 57).

The third general effect has been that 'the expansion of technology has radically altered the character of work.' For the greater part of man's history, work has been a strenuous physical activity, largely carried on alone or in small groups in the open air, requiring considerable dexterity to match human strength to the infinite variations of the natural environment, and culminating in an end product as unambiguously identifiable as the grain in the field or the cloth on a loom (Heilbroner, 1970, p. 93).

The Industrial Revolution profoundly changed the attributes of work. Work now consists more and more of repetitive movements which, however exhausting after a full day, rarely involved more than a fraction of the human being's full muscular ability. In place of the judgments and aptitudes required to meet the variations of nature, work now demanded only the ability to repeat single tasks adapted to a changeless work surface. No longer alone in nature, the worker performed his task in vast sheds with regiments like himself. And most wrenching of all, in place of 'her/his' product, what s/he saw emerging from the factory was an object in which s/he could no longer locate, much less appreciate, her/his own 'deserving' contribution (Heilbroner, 1979, p. 93).

In Sweden, new working methods were introduced that have become prevalent in the primary industry. The old form of lead type-setting has almost disappeared. The new computer-based technology of photo-setting increasingly led to changes in working practices (Wadensjö, 1979, p. 57).

The ultimate question then is the following: What has been the effect on workers of such basic alterations in the place and pattern of labor? When one looks at factories and offices, s/he finds that industrial technology often subjects women or men to a stultifying and enervating discipline that makes work a singularly joyless and meaningless process to which they must subordinate their individual personalities. It is an aspect of technology that has disturbed observers since Adam Smith commented two hundred and more years ago that a human being who endlessly performed the same task 'generally becomes stupid and ignorant as it is possible for a human creature to become.' Karl Marx later on asserted with passion and perception the terrible effects of industrial capitalism in divorcing the worker from the fruits of her/his own toil (Heilbroner, 1979, pp. 93-94).

Whether or not further technological innovation, as proposed by the OECD, was the best strategy for Sweden to get itself out of the 'socio-economic trap' is not very clear in subsequent literature. However, Heilbroner's conclusion on the general question of the impact of technology on society is appropriate here.

> Man is certainly as much the servant and the master of his industrial apparatus. Yet we must guard against too easy an indictment of technology as the great dehumanizer. Let us not forget the terrible toll on its exhausted peasants and its brutalized common laborers. Further, let us bear in mind that if the repressive and disciplinary aspects of technology predominate in our time, it may be because we are still only in the inception of the industrial history of humankind. In a longer perspective, this same technology holds forth at least the promise of an eventual emancipation of man, as machinery gradually takes over his onerous tasks (Heilbroner, 1979, p. 94).

Indeed, making a choice among highly competitive alternatives is never a simple exercise. And the more complex the alternatives, the more the decision-making process will impact other issue areas since major sacrifices must be made in a world of scarcity.

The LO Suggestion

LO saw the stagflation in Sweden during the 1970s and the 1980s as a consequence of the concentration of the ownership of capital. The organization, therefore, also saw its primary task as to resolve or at least reduce the conflict between trade union solidarity and, for purposes of redistribution policy, to restrain the profits of successful enterprises. The second of the LO's objectives was 'to check the concentration of wealth among traditional groups of owners,' which was the inevitable concomitant of industrial self-financing. Noting that this situation was merely one part of the problem of the unequal distribution of wealth in Sweden, LO did not propose to concern itself with the wider question of ownership and with taxation of individual persons through wealth, gift and inheritance taxes and capital gain tax, but to confine itself to the narrower question of industrial ownership. Not only was this part of the solution where inequality was very much in evidence, it was also one of major strategic significance. LO, therefore, aimed at achieving three important goals. They were: (1) equity, (2) distribution, and (3) increased employee influence over the economic sphere (Meidner, 1978, pp. 14-15).

LO envisioned a common element among the three aims, since they were all concerned with distribution policy. There was a fear that if wage solidarity was successful, it would have led to an unintended shift between the incomes of capital and labor to the detriment of the latter. Industrial expansion would have largely taken place via self-financing, which would then have meant that the increase in assets (a prerequisite for growth and progress) would have accrued only to the owners of capital. Intensive changes in the economic structure, noted LO, would have accentuated the concentration of ownership and, thus, of power (Meidner, 1978, p. 15).

The organization contended that there was nothing new in this, since wage solidarity had been pursued in Sweden for years. It was indicated that capital growth via self-financing had been in existence. The process of industrial concentration was an obvious consequence of constant changes in the economic structure, the scope of which was demonstrated in official studies for many years. The concentration of economic power, also a problem of distribution, is a phenomenon which had long been noticed and discussed. What was new, LO contended, was that these problems were more and more being experienced as central or key issues and they had been drawn into the spotlight which had long been shining on other issues such as inflation, the structure of the economy, and intensive social reform work. The discussion of the 1971 Congress and LO's subsequent remit indicated that a fundamental social question of distribution had again become topical, and also that trade unionists had begun to see some connection between capital formation and the amount of influence which employees had over industrial life (Meidner, 1978, pp. 15-16).

LO maintained that the objectives which it had set out were identifying something more than a trade union concern alone. Other concerns it noted included, first and foremost, the demand for full employment. It argued that the achievement of this most important and fundamental of all aims must not be prejudiced by any policies of reform towards redistribution. Closely related to this aim was the demand for a high level of capital formation. The organization further maintained that this aspect was an essential condition for high and rising employment. The Swedish economy, the LO noted, was very exposed to foreign competition, and a high investment ration must, therefore, be accordingly sustained in order to defend Sweden's position in foreign markets. Probably few trade unions were as positive as the Swedish ones in their attitudes toward a high level of investment to the steady expansion of technological regeneration of the apparatus of production. This can be attributed not solely to a ready appreciation of economic relationships but primarily to a successful employment and labor market policy. LO further maintained that its mission should be the recommendation of a higher level of capital formation (Meidner, 1978, pp. 16-17). But, nevertheless, the LO assumption was a fairly obvious one: its solutions must not exacerbate the problems of providing investment which the authorities would have considered desirable.

Another important stipulation made by the LO was that any attempts to meet its three main objectives should be neutral with respect to costs, wages, and prices. A measure of distributive policy which imposed a cost burden on enterprises could conceivably be shifted on to prices and be inflationary without at the same tome achieving any real redistributive effect. It also follows that wage policy must not be prejudiced, and wage bargaining must be assumed to exploit to the full extent the possibilities for saving and consumption (Meidner, 1978, p. 17).

LO further emphasized that finding an arrangement which reinforced solidarity in wage policy must finally satisfy the obvious condition that it did not run counter to the main aim of that policy, which was to equalize incomes between different groups of employees. This meant that any power-sharing scheme which gave rise to new disparities in income within the total aggregate of employees would not have been acceptable to the trade union (Meidner,

1978, p. 17). What mechanisms would the LO had employed to stop such new disparities from happening and what it would do if they do happen were not discussed. Thus, at this point, a review of the work by Himmelstrand and his partners on the Wage-earners' Fund and the contradiction of mature capitalism (1982) will be quite suggestive, since it encompasses many of the arguments proffered in support of and against the LO suggestion.

In relation to the question of the Fund and the contradiction between capital and labor, Himmelstrand and company stressed that the accumulation of capital under the direct or indirect control of private capitalists was a result of supply-demand relations setting the prices on commodity and factor markets. Labor only retained that part of its fruits of labor which was needed for its reproduction at a level determined by the success of previous wage struggle by socially accepted standards of living, which also were the result of previous struggle, and by what organized labor could twist out of the hands of private capital given prevailing conditions on the factor and commodity markets (Himmelstrand et al., 1982, p. 289). The major question then was the following: How could such a contradiction be eliminated, or at least be reduced?

It was suggested that if large companies were to be required by law to issue shares amounting to 20 per cent of yearly profits to the Wage-earners' Fund, this would have meant that surplus appropriated by capital would be appropriated by labor. By definition, this implied a successive elimination of the contradiction between labor and capital, as labor increasingly reappropriated and took control over an increasing position of the accumulated capital (Himmelstrand et al., 1982, p. 290).

However, it should be cautioned that even though this was a conclusion true by definition, some complications could have emerged when one moves from the level of definition to the wider context of social relations of production and considering possible capital countermoves. One of these could have been that the reappropriation of capital by labor could have led to an increasingly bureaucratic or technocratic union control over capital rather than a more democratic control with a high degree of workers' participation in union affairs.

On this possibility, it was suggested that because of Sweden's past examples, it could not be seen how the contradiction between capital and labor would become greater, even with a bureaucratically managed system of the Wage-earners' Fund than with ordinary private capitalism. Another countermove would then be the possibility that capitalists, in order to evade the effects of legislation on the Wage-earners' Fund, could restructure large companies which did not reach the threshold of 500 employees as a starting point for the issuing of wage-earners' shares as indicated in the LO-SAP report. For multinational corporations, it was also possible to evade the obligation to issue wage-earners' shares by taking out all or most of their profits and sending them to branches abroad. It was argued that because of the political reality inherent in Sweden, such a serious complication would not occur because the labor movement remains very well conscious and organized, not only in unions but also in political activity (Himmelstrand et al., 1982, pp. 290-291). But such an answer is rather simplistic in the sense that no system should place its entire trust on 'past' political relations (between LO and the government) when it comes to the formulation of a 'future' path that would affect millions of lives.

Another issue that arose was that of the Fund and the contradiction between forces and relations of production. It was assumed that in mature capitalism, social relations of production remained private in character, whether corporate or personal interests were involved, while productive forces had become increasingly social or even international in character. In other words, there was a mismatch between forces and relations of production in mature capitalism. The question here was whether the Wage-earners' Fund would imply a change of the relations of production, making them more social in character so as to match the increasingly social character of productive forces. It was suggested that to answer a question of this magnitude was to take into account not only the role of the Wage-earners' Fund on the level of simple enterprises but the interlocking of this level with what was done on higher regional, social and international level of political action and control. Socialization of the realities of production implied the involvement of broader social interests than those represented at the level of single enterprises. It was, thus, maintained that the operation of the Wage-earners' Fund, already at the level of single enterprises at the time, would help to assure a production satisfying broader social interests than private capitalist can do (Himmelstrand et al., 1982, pp.291-292).

With respect to the Fund and market self-determination, it was noted that the tendency of competitive markets to self-destruct over time through the contradiction and centralization of private capital resulted from the operation of market forces themselves. In socialism, it was noted that this contradictory character of the competitive market is resolved by eliminating the market as a social reality and by replacing it with presumably consistent central planning and regulation. Citing the example of the GOSPLAN (the central planning agency of the Soviet Union), it was maintained by Himmelstrand and his partners that central planning could certainly have made use of the 'theoretical model' of market forces even in the absence of competitive market processes in order to determine prices and the optimal allocation of resources (Himmelstrand et al., 1982, pp. 295-296). Despite the fact that prices of goods were relatively low and stable in the Soviet Union, the GOSPLAN also meant long lines at shopping areas and shortages of consumer goods. Even though it is true that Swedes are not new to queuing, but to what extent would they tolerate it? Moreover, could Swedes with their luxurious tastes afford to suffer shortages of certain consumer goods to which they have become accustomed?

In addition, it was argued that a system of wage-earners' funds, supplemented with necessary regional and national political interventions, would seem to maintain and develop competition on commodity markets while preventing the destructive market concentration and centralization nature of private capital (Himmelstrand et al., 1982, p. 297).

Looking at the aspect of the Fund and the destruction of incentive structures, it was held that the incentives which are the psychological mainsprings of the capitalist system tend to be destroyed by the intermittent fall of the rate of profit. Its intermittent and far from universal character implies that this destruction of incentives is only partial and less likely, for instance, in concentrated multinational corporations minimally exposed to international competition that are capable of mark-up pricing to attain target profits. But the tendency is widespread enough to have serious repercussions on incentives for investments in the capitalist order. It was also noted that incentives for work and for increasing private consumption also seem to approach a ceiling in mature capitalism and do become less salient than other incentives related to needs for other qualities of life and work than those offered by a capitalist consumer society. The incentive structure of work in capitalist enterprises shapes the worker into a passive risk-minimizer rather than into an active and innovative producer (Himmelstrand et al., 1982, p. 297).

To this position, claim was made that a fully fledged system of wage-earners' funds which would involve a high degree of workers' self-management could be expected to change these failing incentive structures of private capitalism at several levels. This assumption was borne out of the belief that, firstly, one can expect the profit elasticity of investments to be less within a system of wage-earners' funds than in private capitalism. Secondly, that qualitative incentives competing with the quantitative incentives of a consumer society can find more natural outlets in labor-controlled enterprises by self-managed improvements which are difficult to attain in a system mainly geared to private accumulation of capital. And thirdly, that the destructive incentive structure of positive risk-minimization in work under private capitalism is less likely to dominate in labor-controlled enterprises. Active and innovative workers will be more common, even if the system cannot guarantee that every worker exhibits such traits (Himmelstrand et al., 1982, pp. 297-298). And, of course, such an answer to a question of this magnitude is rather insufficient, especially when one considers past and current experiences of the interplay of consumers or shareholders' concerns in a given economic activity.

Given the preceding discussion, it is not farfetched to suggest that in dealing with the Apartheid system, Sweden also had to consider its own 'sustainability,' à la Lester Brown (1981). In light of such a reality, Sweden, like any other country operating in the Capitalist world system, would be challenged to change and adapt. Despite the fact that public policy would play a central role in Sweden's anti-Apartheid stance, it would be more effective if augmented by the adjustment process to the central role also played by market forces. Some policy instruments would have to be sharpened, some retired, and some created to fit the changing contours of circumstances and social will.

Relations with Other Western/Capitalist States

As mentioned earlier, many scholars of Scandinavian politics have supported the contention that Sweden has a close relationship with other Western/Capitalist states. And if one is to accept the notion that the foreign policy of any state is influenced both by internal and external factors, then, the relationship between Sweden and the other Western/Capitalist states becomes an imperative area of concern in this exercise.

This is especially important because we live in an interdependent world. And the issue of global interdependence had long since been dealt with quite well by Robert O. Keohane and Joseph S. Nye in their book, *Power and Interdependence* (1977). After reviewing the propositions rendered by both the 'traditionalists' and the 'modernists' on the issue of global interdependence, Keohane and Nye then went on to present complementary approaches for grasping the essence and reality of interdependence in contemporary world politics. While there is no room in this exercise to present these approaches, the curious reader can be well served by reading the entire book.

However, one of the important questions raised by Keohane and Nye ('What are the major features of world politics when interdependence, particularly economic interdependence, is extensive?') (1977, p. 5) can be directed to Sweden. A review of some developments in Sweden's foreign policy history will be useful to examine such a question.

Sweden's foreign policy up to the end of the 19th Century was the personal affair of the monarch. Before this period, Sweden switched its alliance between powers that it perceived to better serve its interests. But because of its growing fear of Russia (once its ally), Sweden adopted the policy of neutrality (Andersson and Weibul, 1980, pp. 41-43). This policy served Sweden quite well by keeping it out of the two world wars.

While Sweden remained neutral even after those wars, a new global system was established due to the collapse of the United Kingdom's (UK) imperialist system. This new system, labeled 'bipolar,' emerged out of the hostility between the United States and the USSR. In the Capitalist West, America's military and political dominance helped to strengthen the Western alliance. In the Socialist/Communist East, the Soviet Union created the Socialist Alliance.

Nonetheless, as Sweden continued to maintain that its foreign policy was neutral, those critical of the policy frequently questioned its sincerity. The incident in which Swedish government officials were publicly exposed for encouraging the experimentation of nuclear weapons was a case in point. As Gwyne Dyer, a columnist for *The Washington Post*, based in London, England revealed, it was a widely held belief by many that 'Sweden is secretly one of NATO's (North Atlantic Treaty Organization) neutrals–more distant from the Western Alliance than other Scandinavian countries like Denmark that loiter just inside the door, but nevertheless really a NATO associate' (Dyer, 1985, p. 11A).

This perception may be explained by the fact that, in spite of its neutralist claim, Sweden shares with the United States certain bonds that keep the two countries politically and economically closer to each other. These are: (a) Like the United States, Sweden has been progressive in its development of a modern political system and a freer society since the 19th Century. (b) During the 19th Century, a large number of Swedish peasants (about 850,000) left their homeland for new settlements in America. The kin of these Swedish-Americans have today become some of the most politically and economically successful Americans (a good example of such success is John Anderson who ran for the presidency of the USA as an independent candidate in 1980–and because of his Swedish roots, Anderson received a great deal of media coverage and moral support in Sweden). (c) The United States and Sweden have shared a very healthy trade relationship over the years (Bangura, 1987, p. 132).

These bonds between the United States and Sweden stretch way back to the 17th Century when the first Swedish settlements took shape in America and now embrace millions of Americans of Swedish descent. King Gustav II Adolf's vision to establish a Swedish colony across the Atlantic never bore fruits, but six years after his death, in 1638, groups of Swedes and Finns were sent to Delaware. These groups introduced the log cabin which became the prominent home-building pattern and social symbol of the American frontier. Their plight for a colony was overwhelmed by the Dutch and then later by the English, but these Swedes and Finns remained in the new world. They blended quite well with the larger society and left their moral and architectural influences upon it. A sober and industrious group, the Swedes up until the end of the 18th Century brought their pastors from Sweden (Scott, 1975, p. 277).

One of the adventurous and freedom-loving Swedish nobles, Axel von Fersen, played an important role in the American Revolution before he became involved with Marie Antoinette (1775-1793), who was the very beautiful queen of France who died on the Guillotine because she helped to undermine the monarchy leading to the French Revolution). In 1768, the Crown Prince of Sweden (who later became Gustav III) was so impressed with Benjamin Franklin's acclaim as a scientist and a 'worthy bourgeois' that the Prince advocated the tailoring of the Swedish school system in line with Franklin's principles laid down for Pennsylvania (Scott, 1975, p. 278).

The Swedish settlers on Delaware did make lasting marks on American history. John Hanson, for example, a descendant of those early Swedish emigrants became the first president of the United States Congress. Another Swede, Nils Collin, who was the last of the pastors sent from Sweden, founded the famous Historical Society of Pennsylvania. In addition, the 'American letters' sent home by ardent Swedish pioneers bragged and romanticized about their new home. For example, Gustaf Unonius, the founder of the Swedish settlement at Pine Lake, Wisconsin, wrote about America as follows:

Work, and honest occupation, is no disgrace. Conventional prejudices, class interest, meanest of public opinion, tyranny of fashion are not present to hamper every step. Why should I not go to America, to that country which booms like a shining Eldorado before the eyes of every adventurous youth, to that country whose fabulous history compelled our attention from our earliest years at school. That country which has become the grave of old prejudices, a cradle for the true liberty and equality and principles of social beneficence for new generations (Scott, 1975, p. 280).

However, Unonius later had to return to Sweden to argue against emigration to America following his years of hardship and disappointment in Wisconsin. He later stated in his memoirs that his two great mistakes in life were: (1) going to America and (2) leaving it (Scott, 1975, p. 280).

The mass movement of Swedes to America also helped to transform the old country. In the early 20th Century, Swedish industrial and agricultural employers became worried about the draining of Swedish society. E. H. Thonberg, a sociologist, assisted in the great Emigration Inquiry of 1907-1913 and stated openly that: 'we reformers used (emigration) as a vehicle for social legislation.' Andrian Molin, a right-winger, worked very hard to promote individual home-ownership in Northern Sweden in order to keep potential emigrants at home (Scott, 1975, p. 288).

These developments also led to good diplomatic relations between the two countries. In 1783, the United States signed its first treaty with a non-belligerent state (Sweden). The treaty was signed because both countries wanted to maintain the freedom of the seas in order to further international trade (Scott, 1975, p. 289).

But as hinted earlier, in spite of the bonds that bind these two countries, the United States and Sweden have experienced difficulties in their relations. And a good example of this was the Vietnam War issue. At the height of the war, the then Prime Minister of Sweden, Olof Palme, became very critical of the American role in Vietnam. What American policy-makers found offensive in Palme's criticisms was his placing of the United States' bombing of Vietnam in the same category as outrages committed by the USSR, Nazi Germany and South Africa through the years. Palme's criticisms prompted the American government to recall its Charge d'Affaires and to send the new Swedish Ambassador back to Sweden in 1973. But as Palme claimed, his act was not one of anti-Americanism. During an interview with an American journalist, Palme explained the rationale for his criticisms as follows: 'My attitude toward the United States has always been very positive. I was educated there, I love the country and I love the people, so I have never been against the United States. I have been against the Vietnam War which I think is completely out of line with the American tradition' (United States Congress, 1973, pp. 3-4).

However, even at the height of the disagreement, the American public had a high regard for Sweden and its people. As the ORC Caravan Surveys presented to the House Committee on Foreign Affairs during the hearings on 'US Diplomatic Relations with Sweden' on September 12, 1973, revealed,

1. Forty six per cent of Americans believed that Sweden would be a good country in which to live; only 14 per cent did not think they would like to live there.

2. Overall, Americans saw Sweden as a technologically advanced, aesthetically pleasant country whose citizens are well taken care of by their government.

3. Sweden's criticism did not damage Sweden's reputation among Americans. Fewer than one American in ten believed that Sweden's

opposition to United States Southeast Asia policies was an expression of anti-American feelings.

4. A large majority of community leaders knew that Sweden had opposed US involvement in Vietnam. However, the bulk of the American public was not sure about Sweden's position on USA's involvement in Vietnam.

5. When Sweden granted young men from the United States permission to stay in Sweden to avoid serving in Vietnam, a majority of the community leaders who were interviewed (55 per cent) approved of the fact that Sweden offered shelter to such Americans. However, among the American public, more people were against Sweden granting shelter (43 per cent) than in favor (27 per cent).

6. Before they learned that the Swedish Information Service was sponsoring the surveys, community leaders ranked four European countries (Sweden, France, Switzerland and Poland) on a series of questions. Sweden was ranked first for taking the best care of its people. Sweden and Switzerland ranked first for political freedom and having the most highly educated people. France and Sweden were considered to have the most advanced technology. But France and Sweden ranked behind Switzerland for being the best friend of the USA (United States Congress, 1973, p. 12).

Nonetheless, no matter the strains in their relations, Sweden and the United States have continued to interchange people, ideas and goods. When problems arise between them, they engage in frank discussions, even though some of the discussions turn out to be quite heated. What is important is that both countries try to understand each other.

However, on the issue at hand, Apartheid, Sweden and the United States with some other Western/Capitalist states played fundamentally different roles. While Sweden was vehemently opposed (see discussion in Chapters 1, 2 and 3), but cautious in its dealings with South Africa, the United States with some other Western/Capitalist states were for a very long time quite supportive of the Apartheid regime, as reflected in their anti-Apartheid voting records at the UN (Bangura, 1987, p. 138). This support continued especially at a time when Sweden was calling for stringent economic sanctions against the Pretoria government.

Again, in spite of their differing positions on Apartheid, trade between the United States and Sweden continued to play a significant role in their overall relations. And this was very important to Sweden, if not the USA. The importance of foreign trade to Sweden was very well captured by one of the well-known Swedish scholars, Nils Andrén, when he posited that the way Sweden reacted to international issues, besides other factors, depended on Sweden's economic interests in its capacity as an exporting nation (1982, p. 77).

Relations with Communist/Socialist States

Once an ally of Russia, it was the massive military build up of Russia in the 19th Century that eventually led Sweden to pursue its policy of neutrality. Sweden's fear of Russia's military build up was legitimate, given some of its historical experiences with the Russians. For example, Russia won its first naval victory when it took its expansionist war into Swedish waters and subsequently invaded the Swedish mainland. The Russian ruler, Peter the Great, was able to force Sweden to recognize his Baltic territorial gains by the signing of the Treaty of Nystadt in 1721. The treaty was signed after more than twenty years of intermittent but bitter warfare that came to be known as the 'Great Northern War.' This war enabled Russia to state its claim as an European power (Reshetar, Jr., 1978, p. 4).

By 1807, Alexander I of Russia decided to support Napoleon in his wars. Alexander's support made it possible for Russia to take Finland away from Sweden, making it a Russian Grand Duchy in 1809. This victory over Sweden inspired the Russians in 1812 to acquire Bessarabia from the Ottoman Empire. And by 1815, Russia turned against Napoleon, enabling it to acquire 'Congress Poland' along with Warsaw (Reshetar, Jr., 1978, p. 5).

But just as the Swedes had been critical about the USSR's continued military build up, so had the Soviets about Sweden's own military industry. As Andrén pointed out, the USSR raised critical voices on various contexts of Sweden's security policy. Soviet government officials consistently warned Swedish government officials of the consequences for 'unsatisfactory defense' of Sweden's airspace against violations from cruised missiles. These warnings were heightened especially at the time when attention was focused on Eurostrategic weapons (Andrén, 1982, p. 50).

Andrén also noted that Lev Voronkov, a Soviet author and scholar at the Soviet Academy of Economics and International Relations, criticized the Swedes for having a weak defense system against nuclear weapons. But at the same time, *Pravada* was accusing Sweden of participating in the arms race because of its increased spending on defense activities. This led Andrén to suggest that the Soviet criticisms did not form a consistent pattern, but they were all directed against important aspects of Swedish security policy. Furthermore, he noted that what was not being stated by the Soviets was the ease with which they had been able to violate Swedish territorial waters (1982, p. 52). A good example was the case of the 'Whiskey on the Rocks'–the lone Soviet submarine that got stuck between the rocks on a Swedish beach in 1982.

Another fear of the Swedes was the one pointed out by Andrén in Johan Jorgen Holst's book, *Five Roads to Nordic Security* (1973). That particular fear had to do with two strategically very important areas in the hands of the Nordic states: One is the area between the Baltic and the North Sea, which includes both the Oresund, the Belts, and the straits between Denmark and the south of Norway. The other area is the 'Nordic Cap,' one that is vulnerable climatologically and strategically and was closer to the Soviet naval bases in the Murmask area. Also, the USSR had increased its efforts in establishing naval bases on most of the Seven Seas (Andrén, 1973, p. 133).

Thus, given its geographical proximity to the USSR, Sweden was conscious of its vital strategic position between the East and the West, and it decided to maintain its policy of neutrality. But Sweden's neutrality did not hamper its ability to criticize the belligerent actions of the superpowers. This was exemplified by Sweden's protests over the USSR's intervention in Czechoslovakia. During several public demonstrations in Stockholm (the largest ever in Swedish history) in 1968, Sweden's Foreign Minister, Nilsson, denounced 'the Soviet Union's brutal aggression against Czechoslovakia' (United States Congress, 1973, p. 4).

And throughout the 1970s, Sweden continuously demonstrated its disappointment toward the Soviet Union for its military actions in Afghanistan. Besides public denunciations, Sweden's political parties boycotted the Soviet-sponsored Communist conference in Paris in April 1980. The boycott, which was followed by few other countries, did not sit well with the Kremlin because it was the first meeting of its kind to be held outside of an Eastern-bloc state (Nogee and Donaldson, 1984, p. 243).

But as mentioned earlier, Sweden's neutrality policy raised many doubts and questions among the Soviets. One question that was frequently asked was the following: If Sweden was neutral in the true sense of the word, why had it amassed so great a military capability given its geographical proximity to the Soviet Union (Swedish Institute, 1982). The response that was frequently provided by Swedish government officials was best summed up by Andrén when he asserted the following:

> If you are threatened, you should either be strong or have friends willing to help you. The paradox is that if you are weak you are unlikely to find friends, and if you are sufficiently strong, you will hardly need them. A neutral country may have friends but can never rely completely on their assistance in terms of need. Strength borrowed from other powers is not automatically available. Credibility must be built on the nation's own strength (1982, p. 24).

The Swedish Institute, in its *Fact Sheet Sweden* (1982), subtitled 'The Swedish Defense System,' reported that Sweden's policy of neutrality and the will of the Swedes to preserve their national integrity necessitated a strong defense that aimed at (a) a 'total defense'–embracing the entire population; (b) a 'military defense'–that involves the armed forces; and (c) a 'civil,' 'economic' and 'psychological' defense. To this end, Sweden's armed forces, which consisted of army, naval and air services, had over 850,000 men. Since the end of World War II, four to five per cent of the Swedish GDP had been spent on the country's military defense each year.

While Sweden and the USSR had differences over the years on certain issues, Sweden, nevertheless, continued its advocacy for detente between the East and the West. Sweden saw such a policy as a rational and realistic approach for all nations on this planet. Quite appropriately, Sweden did its best to have a healthy relationship with the USSR. Indeed, the two countries had a healthy trade relationship over the years, from a low of $100 million (in total trade) in 1960 to a high of about $1.5 billion in 1979 (Bangura, 1987, p. 144).

Furthermore, Sweden and the Communist/Socialist states shared the same sentiments on the issue of Apartheid. These countries regarded the South African system to be a threat to international peace and security. They together, therefore, called on the international community to impose comprehensive and stringent economic, political and social sanctions on the South African government, and they also continued to give varied forms of support to the liberation forces striving to change the status quo in South Africa. And while Swedish development assistance to Southern Africa was directed toward the purpose of helping individuals, liberation groups and governments of the region to withstand and counteract South Africa's Apartheid system, the Soviet Union took and called for even much harsher steps. The USSR had no diplomatic or economic dealings with South Africa, and it continued to undermine Pretoria's presence in Namibia. As the former Soviet Minister of Foreign Affairs, Andrei Gromyko, stressed at the 39th session of the UNGA, 'There can be no doubt, however, that the Namibian people will find freedom and independence. The colonist policy of South Africa and its protectors is, in the modern world, an historically doomed anomaly' (ILO, 1985, pp. 109-110).

And just as Sweden had put the blame for the continued survival of the Apartheid system squarely on the 'moral laps' of Western/Capitalist states (refer to the discussion in the introductory chapter), so had the USSR and its Eastern bloc allies. As Gerogi Gyrov, the Socialist Governments of Eastern Europe and Asia representative (a member of the Nationalist Committee for Solidarity with the Peoples of Asia and Africa) to the UN-OAU Conference held on Oslo in 1973, stated,

> Foreign monopolies are trying to get maximum profits from the situation (in South Africa) to the detriment of the indigenous inhabitants. The moral, political and military support from countries like the Federal Republic of Germany, the United Kingdom, the United States and other members of NATO has been more direct and has been increasing in volume... (Stoke and Winstrand, 1973, p. 218).

Thus, Gyurov suggested that the Soviet Union, the Socialist countries and other forward-looking peoples of the world should continue to support all forms of effective assistance to those South African liberation groups that were fighting for their 'independence, freedom, self-determination and equal rights' (Stoke and Winstrand, 1973, p. 218). He also stressed the fact that the Socialist bloc supported all forms of armed struggle against the Pretoria regime. The was because, as Gyurov put it, the Socialist bloc recognized 'the right of the oppressed and colonial peoples to use all means, including armed struggle, to throw off the yoke of colonialism. Fighting with arms is part of one's legitimate right of self-defense against colonialism' (Stoke and Winstrand, 1973, p. 218). Therefore, in spite of their differences on certain issues, Sweden and the USSR shared a healthy trade relationship and wanted to see an immediate end to the Apartheid system in South Africa (Bangura, 1987, p. 146).

Relations with Apartheid South Africa

As pointed out earlier, Sweden was vehemently opposed to the Apartheid system, but it was not willing to suffer a severe loss in its economic dealings with South Africa. While South Africa was of secondary importance to Sweden's overall foreign trade, Swedes working for Swedish companies that did business with and in South Africa lived quite pleasant lives. And Swedish-South African trade, besides few minor declines, experienced dramatic increases over the years–from a low of $25 million in 1960 to a peak of $250 million in 1981. This made South Africa important to Sweden (Bangura, 1987, p. 147).

The trade relations between the two countries, therefore, became especially important to Swedish policy-makers given the country's post-war economic policy. That policy, according to Assar Lindbeck, and as pointed out earlier, was to increase the number of policy targets, and full-employment became the main target. However, he also noted that since the late fifties, as economic growth became the 'holy cow' in other countries, Sweden also turned its attention to the growth rate. And during the early 1960s, problems such as regional balance and environmental concerns shifted the emphasis to income and wealth distribution. Meanwhile, the full-employment target took on several faces: increasingly it had 'been applied not only to the labor market as a whole, but to various sub-markets, such as married women; the handicapped; employees in individual branches and specific regions, etc' (Lindbeck, 1973, p. 23).

Thus, even though Sweden provided aid to the front-line states and liberation forces opposed to Pretoria's rule, it also increased its trade and continued its diplomatic relations with South Africa in order to further its economic policy. This duality hinged on the fact that Sweden was pushing for comprehensive economic sanctions on South Africa that should have included the entire international community, instead of taking unilateral actions. As an ILO report illustrated, by tradition, Sweden participated in sanctions against another country only after such measures had been decided upon or recommended by the UNSC. Thus, Sweden repeatedly called upon the UNSC to decide on comprehensive, mandatory economic sanctions against South Africa in line with Chapter VII of the UN Charter. Sweden, therefore, argued that because economic sanctions were appropriate measures for peaceful pressure, the UN should waste no time instituting them. In its efforts to speed up economic sanctions against South Africa, Sweden, in 1976, brought forward an UNGA resolution that called for the UNSC to consider effective steps in stopping foreign investments in South Africa, a way to weaken Pretoria's war efforts. Sweden reintroduced the resolution during subsequent sessions of the UNGA and later included the termination of financial loans to South Africa. Other actions supported by Sweden against the Apartheid regime included the following: (a) an arms embargo and, together with other Nordic countries, suggested practical measures that could be taken at the UN to make the embargo more effective; (b) an oil embargo and support for a Norwegian initiative to arrange a conference with the oil-producing and oil-exporting countries (which had declared that they did not want to sell oil to South Africa) in order to make the policy quite effective; (c) financial contributions for a survey on shipment of oil and oil products to South Africa; (d) initiatives on UN specialized agencies to intensify anti-Apartheid actions within their sphere of competence; (e) increased aid through specialized agencies to help the South African liberation movement and the refugees and victims of Apartheid; (f) increased UN pressure on South Africa for Namibia's independence to grant the Namibian people the opportunity to determine their future in free elections under the supervision of the UN in accordance with Resolution 435; and (g) increased humanitarian aid to SWAPO and Namibian refugees to resist South African rule in that country (ILO, 1984, pp. 65-66).

But as already suggested several times in this book, Sweden's continued relations with Pretoria somehow contradicted its anti-Apartheid stance. As the LO/TCO report (cited earlier) pointed out, according to data provided by Sveriges Industriforbund (the Federation of Swedish Industry), Sweden's exports to South Africa were providing jobs for a few thousand Swedes. And that because South Africa had improved as a market, Swedish exports to that country exceeded its imports (from South Africa). Sweden was exporting engineering products, paper pulp, paper and wood products to South Africa, and these goods were very important for Pretoria's industrial expansion. On the import side, Sweden bought different metal alloys, raw materials, fuels and fruits from South Africa. The technology sales to South Africa were taking place in stiff competition with other Western/Capitalist states (LO/TCO, 1975, p. 107).

Furthermore, the report stated that several big Swedish enterprises were firmly entrenched in the South African market. Besides Volvo, which had no subsidiary in South Africa, the Swedish companies that did operate in that country did so quite openly, and they did not mind doing so. Nonetheless, it was also pointed out in the report that Volvo maintained an intimate cooperation with Lawson Motors (a South African company). Under the supervision of Volvo, Lawson Motors assembled some 2,000 Volvo cars and trucks each year. In addition to that, Volvo's representatives in Great Britain had bought up the entire Lawson Motors. Thus, the report argued that

... it is probably that today the general agent is formally, although indirectly, controlled by Volvo, the manager of which company has announced, not without expected publicity effects perhaps, that for political reasons the Company has refrained from establishing itself in the native country of the Apartheid policy. During the Spring of 1975, a managing director has been "lent" to Lawson Motors by Volvo in Sweden. The idea of this is to reorganize the latter firm, which is looked upon as nearly run down (LO/TCO, 1975, pp. 108-109).

However, as an assuagement, the report also stressed that because only a fraction of the South African industry was dominated by Swedish companies, these companies did not play a very important role in the economic activities of South Africa. This was mainly due to the fact that only about 5,500 persons were working for the Swedish manufacturing industry, and between 1,500 to 2,000 persons were working in Swedish sales and marketing organizations operating in South Africa (LO/TCO, 1975, p. 109).

Nonetheless, there were other aspects of the Swedish companies operating in South Africa that agreed with the general Apartheid system in that country. These aspects had to do with wages and other conditions of employment at the Swedish companies. According to Magnusson, white employees in manufacturing jobs earned wages that were four to five times greater than their black counterparts. And these wage gaps between the two groups continued to increase over the years. This was because the starting salaries for whites were considered higher that those for blacks (Magnusson, 1974, p. 44).

Furthermore, Magnusson noted that, like blacks who worked for other companies, those who worked for Swedish companies were paid unsatisfactory wages from the viewpoint of family support. Many of these black families starved and encountered severe material poverty. Their wages did not allow them a materially tolerable existence, and a lot more needed to be done if wage levels for blacks were to reach a point palatable for family support (Magnusson, 1974, p. 44).

But in spite of all this, Magnusson argued that Swedish companies were only operating within the South African societal framework. And thus, according to him,

> In this indirect sense, the Swedish business community supports the politics now dominant in South Africa. No Swedish employer would basically seem to morally sympathize with the South African social order. The indirect support given the apartheid policy by the Swedish business community is a consequence of its being established in that country, and not an expression for a political act of volition (Magnusson, 1974, p. 44).

Magnusson supported this contention by citing generally positive policies employed by Swedish companies in South Africa in order to improve the lot of the non-whites. For example, he cited the fact that SFK introduced a 'book-fund' as a way of providing economic aid to the children of its non-white workers. In 1973, for example, SFK distributed 2,000 Swedish crowns so that

10 children of its workers could pay for school fees and books. And there were plans underway to increase the size of the fund (Magnusson, 1974, pp. 44-45).

Indeed, the foreign policy of a country is a line of action that its government adopts to promote its 'national interests' in the international arena. National interests are the goals and objectives that a country seeks to accomplish. These interests reflect the wants and expectations of the civil society on the one hand, and the aims, wishes, and ambitions of its leaders on the other. Thus, foreign policy represents both the execution of a 'national interest' and the endeavor to accomplish a country's expectations. A foreign policy is usually specific rather than general. More often than not, it exists for only a short period of time. Nevertheless, a country's foreign policy is often based on certain principles, ideas, and ideals that are regarded as an integral part of the country's historical experiences.

The conclusion of World War II witnessed the emergence of the United States and the USSR as preponderant powers in the global arena. Both countries came out of the war with enormous military and technological capabilities. They gradually became the leaders of the so-called Western and Eastern blocs. Middle powers such as Sweden were left to carve out their standing in the international arena by employing strategies that were different from those of the superpowers.

Chapter 5

Sweden's Policy Outcomes

This chapter discusses Sweden's support for the South African liberation movement. The three dimensions of this support included development assistance to the front-line states and the South African liberation forces, Swedish diplomatic missions in the front-line states, and Sweden's anti-Apartheid votes at the UNGA.

Development Aid to the Front-line States and the South African Liberation Forces

Sweden's aid to the front-line states (Angola, Botswana, Lesotho, Malawi, Mozambique, Swaziland, Tanzania, Zambia and Zimbabwe) and the South African liberation forces can be better understood by looking at the issue of international aid in general and that country's (Sweden) aid to the African continent in particular. This is simply because Sweden's aid policy toward liberation movements was generally couched in its relations with the Third World, and its aid policy toward the South African liberation forces and the front-line states was part and parcel of its development policies toward the African continent as a whole.

In her treatise on the issue of development aid in international economic relations, Joan Edelman Spero (1985) suggested that foreign aid was frequently seen by many academics and policy-makers as a means to develop the nations of the South (underdeveloped). The Northern countries (developed) had made public concessional funds their tool for promoting development in the post-war era. Aid was used by Northern countries to maintain the existing international economic order and to win political support from the countries of the South, and it had proved to be a second-best panacea for the economic problems of the South. She also contended that aid had neither changed the nature of North-South relations nor distributed the economic benefit that emerged from these relations. More important, she suggested, was the fact that aid had not been a reliable source of capital and technology for Southern countries because receiving aid was dependent upon the goodwill, political and economic conditions of the Northern states. Spero's discussion highlights the positions of the contending schools of thought on the issue of international development aid in general. The perspectives of these schools can also be placed into two mutually exclusive categories. The first category, which had been dubbed as the *Classical* perspective, saw aid as an important device for development if used properly: that is, if it can promote innovative programs and break those barriers that retard progress. The central theme behind the classical development perspective is the metaphor of *growth*, a powerful concept in Western thought. As Robert Nisbit, for example, suggested,

> of all the metaphors in western thought, the oldest and most powerful is the metaphor of growth. When we say that a culture of constitution or nation 'grows' or 'develops,' ... We are referring to change that is intrinsic to the entity, to change that is held to be as much a part of the entity's nature as any purely structural element (Nisbit, 1969, p. 7).

One of the most popular proponents of this thinking, W. W. Rostow (1960), outlined five stages for economic growth: (1) traditional society, (2) the preconditions for take-off, (3) the take-off, (4) the drive to maturity, and (5) the age of high mass consumption. This strategy owed its conception to the examination of the historical experiences if Western Europe, North America and the Soviet Union.

But as many other scholars pointed out, implicit in the stages of the growth model was the conception that the states in the Third World could also achieve abundance and mass consumption if they followed the same development path the West took to come out of underdevelopment. Furthermore, the growth model suggested that development was a uni-linear process couched in the belief that traditional and modernism were opposite sides of the same coin. But as Andre Gunder Frank aptly argued,

> even a modest acquaintance with history shows that underdevelopment is not original or traditional and that neither the past nor the present of the underdeveloped countries resembles in any important respect the past of the now developed countries. The now developed countries were never *underdeveloped*, though they may have been *undeveloped* (Frank, 1979, pp. 103-104).

Frank's contention hinged on the fact that the experiences of the colonial and underdeveloped states had been quite different from those of the developed countries. Thus, the growth model failed to reflect the history of the underdeveloped world in its proper context.

The second category in the debate over international aid relations is referred to as the *Radical* perspective. The proponents of this school of thought looked at development aid as a tool used by the developed countries to maintain their economic and political domination over the underdeveloped states. The central idea behind this thinking was the concept of *imperialism*. The concept of imperialism as used by contemporary radical scholars was carefully distinguished by Roger Owen and Bob Sutcliffe from the technical sense in which Karl Marx used it to explain the latest mode of capitalist production as a consequence of the working out of its laws of motion: that is, 'principally or exclusively, the relationships between the advanced, imperial country and the colonial or semi-colonial areas falling within its formal or informal empire.' The new use of the concept generally described 'a special stage of capitalist development and, by extension, it speaks of the epoch of imperialism in which this has become the dominant form and stresses the new, distinguishing features of this stage' (Owen and Sutcliffe, 1972, pp. 17-18).

As radical scholars attempted to answer the major question about international aid relations between the developed and the underdeveloped states–i.e. who controlled the development?, theories of 'dependency' became influential in the Third World. Theotonio Dos Santos, for example, defined dependency as a situation whereby 'the economy of certain countries is conditioned by the development and expansion of another economy to which the former is subjected' (Dos Santos, 1970, pp. 231-236). As if by accident or design, the two contending schools of thought discussed here found a home in the discussion on Swedish aid policy toward the underdeveloped states as well. An examination of the debate made it possible to generate the following model into which the available literature on the issue could sensibly be placed (see Table 5.1).

Classical School

The scholars of this perspective envisioned Sweden's aid as a good and necessary source for the development of the poor countries. The Swedish International Development Authority (SIDA), for example, in one of its 1982 reports, asserted that priorities in Swedish development assistance were in the direction of the poorest countries (SIDA, 1982). The gap in this report was that there was no place where a criterion was presented for selecting these 'poorest' countries. And by looking at those African countries that received large amounts of Swedish aid, it was evident that these countries did not represent the poorest on the continent (by the World Bank standards). For example, poorer countries such as Chad and Togo did not receive bilateral aid from Sweden.

Table 5.1 Schools of Thought on Sweden's Aid Policy

Classical School	Radical School
Bhagwati, 1970 Myrdal, 1970 Sida, 1976, 78, 79, 80, 81, 82a, 82b, and 82c Sweden's Ministry of Foreign Affairs, 1981 Ullsten, 1978	Hettne, 1978 Hettne and Wallensteen, 1978 Lindstron, 1971 Miller, 1979 White, 1974

However, Carl Gösta Windstrand and Zdenek Cervenka, in their book, *Scandinavian Development Agreements with African Countries* (1971), suggested that Scandinavian development plans concentrated primarily on the English-speaking countries and on East Africa. The major reason for this, according to the authors, was the fact that English is the first foreign language taught in Scandinavian primary schools. Another reason cited by Windstrand and Cervenka was that, unlike the colonial powers that continued to pursue their interests in their former colonies and trading partners, the Scandinavian states had not followed this pattern (1971, pp. 18-19). While this assessments might have been true for most of the countries that received Swedish aid, it was not true for some. For example, Sierra Leone is an English-speaking country, but it did not fare well in terms of Swedish development aid.

SIDA also maintained that Sweden's program for international development cooperation, as presented in the Budget and Financial Bill for fiscal year 1982/83, equaled just over one percent of the country's (Sweden) estimated Gross Domestic Product (SIDA, 1982). While this might have been quite impressive on the surface, there were some Swedes who raised serious questions about the make-up of the one per cent 'deal.'

As a writer of the *Dagens Nyheter* (Daily News) of September 7, 1983, Kenneth Hermele, reported, toward the end of June, a meeting took place in Paris that ought to have disturbed senses in Stockholm. On June 21, 1983,

Sweden had to answer questions before the 'capitalistic countries' corporation, OECD.' It was the OECD's Aid Committee that had called the meeting to go through Sweden's aid policy. Sweden was chastised; but strange enough, this did not raise eyebrows in Sweden, maintained the writer. Hermele noted that, since a few years back, Sweden had been giving Swedish companies subsidiaries for the aid amount for business with underdeveloped countries. It happened for the fact that the state presented special advantageous credits for the companies' disposition. The credits–that were sometimes called 'mix,' sometimes called 'advantageous,' and later 'laconically' called 'underdeveloped credits'–were a part of Sweden's 'aid,' or, more correctly, 'gift-shares' that helped to fulfill the 'holy' one per cent goal. Whether or not Hermele's contention was valid, SIDA gave no indication of what the make-up of the one per cent deal was to refute the writer's position.

Another point raised by SIDA was that, because of an agency's aspiration to enforce the economic and social development of certain countries and to contribute towards closer relationships between Sweden and some countries, an 'enlarged cooperation' program had been established (SIDA, 1980). Again, no criterion was given for why and how these countries were selected for this special form of assistance. Moreover, when one looks at the African countries that received the enlarged cooperation assistance, Algeria, Egypt, Nigeria, Sudan and Tunisia, one sees that, with the exception of Sudan, the rest of these countries were producers of some form of energy. And considering the fact that a major percentage of Sweden's energy needs was dependent upon imported oil, one could hardly resist the temptation of asserting that Sweden's enlarged cooperation was, at best, aid to help buttress its energy supply.

However, as one of Sweden's highly acclaimed scholars, Gunnar Myrdal, posited, the idea that aid to underdeveloped countries would be in 'the best interest of Sweden does not occur naturally to the Swedes.' The basis for Myrdal's assumption stemmed from the fact that Sweden is not oversized like the United States or the Soviet Union. And 'with somewhat less a puritanical heritage, that particular turn of thought implied in wanting to state every impulse to do a right thing in this selfish way has never become a tradition in Sweden.' Also, because of the fact that Sweden had gone for over a century and a half without war, the author maintained that the 'Swedes in any case do not feel tempted to turn aid into serving the military and strategic interests of Sweden' (Myrdal, 1970, p. 359).

Quite obviously, Myrdal's contention treaded on thin ice since it did not address 'economic self-interests' that could emerge in the name of aid, as Hermele pointed out. As also inferred in the case of 'enlarged co-operation,' a special aid policy of this nature could be assumed to mean an advantageous market relation for the donor country. Therefore, although Myrdal's position on Swedish aid might have been plausible in relation to 'power politics,' it, nevertheless, failed to explain the issue of 'economic self-interest.'

But as Jagdish Bhagwati (1970) maintained, in a time when United States' aid policy was directed toward less development, smaller donors such as Sweden had increased their aid and relaxed the strictness of their lending terms. Bhagwati's assumption was based upon the examination of the volume of aid, as well as the pattern of distribution among recipients. Although the author's quantitative approach explained the increase of Swedish aid to the underdeveloped countries, it did not explain how Swedish lending terms had been relaxed. As a matter of fact, there was no place in the book where Swedish lending terms were examined. And when one considers Hermele's report, again, one begins to doubt the relaxation of Swedish lending terms.

In summary, it is quite evident from the preceding discussion that because of the classical scholars' belief in the Western developmental model and in the 'moral duty' of the developed countries to help the underdeveloped countries, a critical analysis of Swedish aid policy was, thus, sacrificed. Hence, donors such as Sweden whose interests were less clear had usually been satisfied with an uncritical adherence to certain international norms. These difficulties led to a heterodox search for another development paradigm, one that initiated the radical school.

Radical School

The views of the proponents of this school were very well summarized by Björn Hettne. According to him,

> The whole complex of "development aid" may in many respects be regarded as a typical example of quasi-reform. The functions of aid have been many: to make "weak" economies capable of joining the international capitalist market, to make them more able to suppress internal rebellions, to link them to one or the other of the main political blocs and to facilitate the spread of the Western model of development, but rarely to give an impetus to development (Hettne, 1978, p. 25).

As J. D. B. Miller (1979) posited in his essay on international aid, the politics of aid, giving results from the fundamental problem of scarcity, lay at the root of economic effort. And that in the case of Sweden, the country's typical political situation as a parliamentary democracy made it possible for aid programs to enjoy the support of foreign affairs offices and defense departments (because of the influence which it was hoped the programs will provide), by trade and agricultural departments (because it was hoped that aid will be used to buy local goods and in the long-run stimulate demand for such goods on commercial basis), and by humanitarian and church groups (because they wished to improve the lot of their fellow men).

Of Miller's assumptions, the one that the defense departments stood to gain from Swedish aid programs raises some eyebrows. This is because Sweden had no military bases beyond its borders to worry about, and it did not give military assistance to the underdeveloped countries. And it is difficult to see how the defense departments could gain at home from Swedish aid programs. As Stig Lindholm (1971) found out after conducting a scientific investigation and processing pertinent data on Swedish political opinion on the country's aid to underdeveloped countries, there existed very little knowledge and analysis of the policy on the part of Swedes (thus, raising a serious question on Miller's assumption that defense departments enjoyed Swedish public support from the country's aid policy). Such a finding prompted Lindholm to question 'the durability of this solidarity in situations in which more serious sacrifices are required' of the Swedish population.

By way of summary, scholars who saw aid as a tool used by the developed countries to maintain the global economic status quo had, of course, come from the radical end of the political spectrum: the 'neo-Marxist.' Their opposition was directed mainly toward aid from Western countries and rested on the view that Western aid had been an instrument of 'neo-colonialism.' However, the major problem with their argument was the failure to specify just what it was that aid had failed to do. Whether or not they expected aid to be a panacea to the problems of the underdeveloped countries could not be ferreted out of their arguments.

Given these contending views, what then was Sweden's record on aid to African countries and, especially, on aid to the front-line states and the South African liberation forces? According to Windstrand and Cervenka, the Swedish bilateral aid program was inaugurated in 1952 when the Central Committee for Swedish Technical Assistance to Less Developed Countries was established. Its first function involved assistance to the Ethio-Swedish Institute of Building Technology after an agreement was signed between Sweden and Ethiopia in 1954. By 1961, Swedish aid totaled $23.2 million; and when Government Bill No. 100 was passed in the Riksdag, Sweden's aid amount to the underdeveloped countries reached $25.1 million. A new Bill (Kungl. Majits Proposition 1968: 100 of May 28, 1968) was adopted six years later to expand the official assistance to one per cent of the GDP in fiscal year 1974/1975 (Windstrand and Cervenka, 1971, p. 14). Indeed, the front-line states and the South African liberation forces received a reasonably large amount of this

Swedish aid. As a geopolitical group, these front-line states and the liberation forces averaged $74.0 million per year from 1960 to 1984. The group also received more aid than all the other African regional, geopolitical groupings put together during the same period (Bangura, 1987, p. 167). Thus, no matter which school of thought might have appeared more plausible in explaining Sweden's development aid to the front-line states and the South African liberation forces, the main concern in this book is with the magnitude of the aid vis-a-vis Sweden's overall support for anti-Apartheid.

Consequently, at least one major question remains to be explored: that is, what are the effects of Sweden's development aid on the front-line states and the South African liberation forces? The question is so difficult that it is beyond the scope of this book. This is because investigating this question requires many control variables for which data should be collected, mainly because the economic well-being and the struggle of the anti-Apartheid movement did not depend solely on Swedish aid. Nonetheless, it will not be erroneous to speculate that an average aid amount of $74.0 million a year (from 1960 to 1984) would have some positive effects on the liberation struggle. Besides, the very fact that Sweden (a country that is greatly respected around for its morality) gave to the liberation movement added to the legitimacy of the struggle.

But in spite of the shortcoming of being unable to scientifically examine the possible effects of Sweden's development aid to the front-line states and the South African liberation forces, one other question looms to the discussion: that is, what did Sweden expect to gain from its liberation support? Put differently, did Sweden expect to capture massive trade advantage by supporting those groups which it perceived as potential power-brokers when the white regime in South Africa collapsed? Even though any response to this question would, at best, be speculative, it is, nevertheless, worth examining. For as Teresa Hayter, in her book, *Aid as Imperialism* (1971), asserted, 'Aid has never been an unconditional transfer of financial resources. Usually the conditions attached to aid are clearly and directly intended to serve the interests of the governments providing it. For example, aid must generally be used to buy goods and services from its provider' (Hayter, 1971, pp. 15-16). She added that, generally, aid was provided to those countries 'whose internal political arrangements, foreign policy alignments, treatment of foreign private investment, debt-servicing record, export policies, and so on are considered desirable, potentially desirable, or at least acceptable, by countries or institutions providing aid, and which do not appear to threaten their interests' (Hayter, 1971, p. 16).

Furthermore, Hayter suggested that behind the cloak for the need to promote economic development in underdeveloped states, supporters of foreign aid had frequently supported some of the conditions that often went with aid. Thus, she argued that the objective of the development activities in the underdeveloped states were either likely to benefit the richer countries or serve their interests; and secondly, some were not (as officially stated, at least). Hence, according to Hayter,

> The subject of aid has been, and presumably will continue to be, peculiarly obfuscated by confusion about objectives. But even supposing an improvement in general standards of living were the only concern of the providers of aid, it could possibly still be argued that some effort should be made by developed countries to ensure that the resources they transferred did actually contribute to the welfare in developing countries, and were not, for example, merely transferred to Swiss bank accounts, especially as aid competes with other claims on resources within industrialized countries (Hayter, 1971, pp. 16-17).

Hayter's work, which examined the operations of the United States Agency for International Development (USAID), the World Bank and the International Monetary Fund (IMF) in Latin America to support her preceding assertions, presents evidence that was neither complete nor coherent in ferreting out those institutions' stated objectives and observed outcomes.

And after the Brandt Commission's Report came out in 1980, Hayter came up with what she called 'An Alternative View to the Brandt Report.' In that book, which she entitled *The Creation of World Poverty* (1981), she contended that, although the concern shown by the Commission about the state of poverty in the Third World might have been genuine on humanitarian grounds, it did not, however, represent the Commission's major concern. The Brandt Report's proposals for more aid to the underdeveloped countries, according to Hayter, were 'primarily concerned with the preservation of the existing world economic order.' Her proposition hinged upon what she referred to as the two differences between the then current and previous perceptions of the poverty problem by the West: 'first, extreme poverty in underdeveloped countries is not seen as a real threat to the survival of the system rather than as something to be dealt with by occasional philanthropic gestures; and second, a response is required to the current crisis in the world economy' (Hayter, 1981, p. 9).

And in a later book (published in 1985) written with Catharine Watson, Hayter and her partner suggested that underdeveloped states were better off without aid, and instead they should pursue policies of greater self-reliance: that is, policies that force those countries to utilize their own resources, especially their lands, in providing the basic human needs of their citizens; and reducing their dependence on international trade, foreign goods and skills

(Hayter and Watson, 1985, pp. 253-154).

However, another rendering of aid was presented by other scholars. For example, John White argued that most people who were disillusioned by the shortcoming of foreign aid had been less than precise in stating what it was that aid was supposed to have accomplished. He added that only those who possessed greater international illusions could have expected aid to serve as a panacea for global poverty. Thus, the 'failure' of aid, according to White, should have been looked at as limitations within which the developed and underdeveloped states were operating (White, 1974, p. 18).

Furthermore, White pointed out that while it was difficult to assert whether or not the underdeveloped states would have achieved higher rates of economic growth with more, less, or without aid, as some of these states did attain higher economic growth rates than they had before–by the end of the 1970s, the underdeveloped states attained average growth rates of five percent. However, the author cautioned that,

> Self-congratulation over the attainment of this target, however, was tempered by the realization that population was growing more rapidly than had been foreseen, at an annual rate of about 2.5 percent, so that half of the increased income had been needed simply to keep more people alive at the same level (White, 1974, p. 19).

Implicit in the preceding views was the overriding notion of foreign aid being a tool for improving the market conditions in the underdeveloped world either for the interests of the richer states (as per Hayter's thesis), or increasing the economic growth rates of the poor states while also benefitting the donor states (as per White's thesis). Thus, the role of international trade becomes paramount in foreign aid relations. And David Blake and Robert Walters have captured this role quite well when they suggested that in order to promote their national and private economic interests in the underdeveloped states, the rich countries will continue their economic aid programs in the Third World. They noted that the scarcity of certain minerals followed by the aftermath of the oil shortages of 1973 and 1974 made the continuation of aid to the underdeveloped countries even more imperative to buttress the rich states' needs for those resources. For example, Blake and Walters noted, Japan provided massive aid to oil-producing states in the Persian Gulf and to Indonesia following the crisis of the Arab oil embargoes in 1973 and 1974 (Blake and Walters, 1976, pp. 132-133).

In addition, the authors pointed out that rich states also used aid to finance their exports to the underdeveloped states. And that Japan and Germany (especially) have used export credits quite extensively in their aid packages to the underdeveloped countries. Thus, Blake and Walters maintained that

> As long as neomercantilism continues to be an important part of the advanced industrial states' overall trade policies, rich states are likely to continue economic assistance to poor states as a means of improving their balance of trade. For example, in the early 1970s about one third of the imports to India, Pakistan, and Indonesia were financed from aid (Blake and Walters 1976:133).

In essence, international trade, as Harold Heck correctly pointed out, has some impact on everyone's life, and it is, therefore, politically and economically significant to a country that participates in it. It has directly been important to a state's ability in creating employment opportunities, 'and fundamental to such international specialization of labor as can be enjoyed in a world whose nations' physical boundaries are in some cases illogical, where nationalistic feelings rest at times on overcharged nationalism, and where political units must strive deliberately for short-term, if not immediate, economic betterment in order to maintain a semblance of political stability' (Heck, 1972, p. 1).

Hence, states trade with each other because, as Franklin Root aptly suggested, there exist a number of mutually interdependent market conditions (each is both a cause and effect) that make such an activity essential. These conditions include (a) absolute international price differences, (b) absolute international cost differences, (c) dissimilar cost ratios within each country, (d) dissimilar factor price ratios, (e) dissimilar factor supply ratios, and (f) dissimilar factor demand ratios. Root, however, stressed that factor supply ratios are the most fundamental links to the causation chain of these conditions (Root, 1973, p. 63).

In light of these conditions, Root, therefore, posited that a given state is able to obtain more goods in order to satisfy the needs and wants of its citizens by engaging in international trade than if it tried to produce all goods at home. International trade, according to him, is 'indirect production': that is, each country combines its factors of production more effectively by specializing in the production of those goods with higher benefits and lower costs. Hence, a country produces for export those goods in which it has a comparative advantage and imports those goods in which it has a comparative disadvantage (Root, 1973, p. 63).

In examining the connection between international aid and trade, therefore, Anindya Bhattacharya suggested that unrestricted trade and aid are legitimate international means to attain economic development in the underdeveloped states. But that if unrestricted trade is stymied by policy measures, foreign aid—because it comprises of lump-sum transfers of incomes from the developed countries' taxpayers—can be seen as superior to unilateral trade interventions by the underdeveloped countries (Bhattacharya, 1976, p. 61).

Bhattacharya, defining *aid* as a means of direct transfer of real resources without loss of real income of the recipient states and *trade* as an exchange than an addition of such resources, argued that trade can never be a perfect substitute for foreign aid. And if trade artificially raises the market price for the products of the underdeveloped countries, then, it becomes identical with aid. The author also claimed that the ideology of the underdeveloped states of trade, not aid, makes little sense in economic terms because trade can never be a substitute for aid (Bhattacharya, 1976, p. 61).

Furthermore, Bhattacharya maintained that the West had become disenchanted about the contribution aid can make to the development process in the Third World because of the exaggerated expectations from aid recipients and the inflated idea about the real cost of aid. And that with the exception of Holland and the Scandinavian states, public opinion in other developed countries was not sensitized to the goals and needs of the underdeveloped states (Bhattacharya, 1976, p. 61). The ultimate questions, then, is (as stated earlier), did Sweden expect to capture massive trade advantages by supporting those groups which it perceived as being power-brokers once the white regime in South Africa collapsed?

Despite the revelation by Hermele (previously stated) that Sweden had been providing special advantageous credits for some of its companies as part and parcel of its aid packages to the underdeveloped countries, there existed no overwhelming evidence to suggest that Sweden stood to gain a great deal when the white regime in South Africa faced prostration. As the Swedish Secretariat for Future Studies revealed, Sweden's principal trade partners were the industrialized Western states. The Secretariat's statistics showed that about 80 percent of Sweden's foreign trade was with the other Western countries, its trade with the underdeveloped states was about 12 per cent, and the remaining six percent was with Eastern Europe and China (Hermele, 1979, p. 25).

The Secretariat's statistics further pointed out that the greater percentage of Sweden's foreign investments were made in other industrialized Western states. Only about 15 per cent of Sweden's total foreign manufacturing subsidiaries and about 20 per cent of the personnel strength of these manufacturing subsidiaries were in the underdeveloped states. And that when Sweden's investments rose relatively steeply in the underdeveloped countries (between 1960 and 1970), most of these investments were in Latin America. By 1970, Argentina, Brazil, India and Mexico were among the twenty largest recipients of Sweden's investments (in terms of total assets in Sweden's manufacturing subsidiaries in the Third World) (Hermele, 1979, p. 30).

The reason for such developments can be traced to Sweden's trade policy in general. Having been a state that mainly supplied iron and forest products during the past centuries, Sweden later manufactured and exported a variety of machinery, transport equipment and other manufactured products in order to meet its high dependency on foreign trade for its economic growth and its long tradition of extensive worldwide economic relations. This explains why almost 40 per cent of the country's industrial products were being sold overseas (Swedish Institute, 1981).

Until the early 1950s, about half of Sweden's exports comprised of raw materials. Since the mid-1950s, however, the proportion of manufactured goods has increased dramatically. This has meant an alteration of the relative proportions of Sweden's two major raw material groups: forestry and mining products. And 'the latter group is taken in its total array, ranging from iron ore and basic metals to metal products, machinery and transport equipment, and thence to professional and scientific instruments, it accounts for more than half of Sweden's exports. The products of all forest-based industries represent about 21 per cent of the value of total exports' (Swedish Institute, 1981).

Thus, the basic objective of Sweden's trade policy has traditionally been the eradication of customs duties and all other trade barriers worldwide. In this respect, Sweden has consistently pushed for efforts to liberalize international trade and has also kept its own tariffs quite low. For example, raw materials are admitted duty-free and the tariffs on imported semi-manufactures are relatively low. In addition to that, Sweden's tariffs on finished goods have been among the lowest in the world (Swedish Institute, 1981).

Because of this set-up, Sweden, therefore, faces two major issues in its trade policy: (1) Sweden seeks the elimination of all trade barriers on a global scale, and (2) Sweden's great dependence on trade with Western Europe has made it imperative for the Swedes to seek closer trade relations with the Europeans (Swedish Institute, 1981). It, therefore, comes as no surprise that Sweden's major trade partners have been the developed states.

The second reason why it is difficult to ascertain the notion that Sweden's liberation support might have been due to its expected gains when the white regime in South Africa collapsed hinges on many indications that revealed genuine Swedish sensitivities to the development processes in the Third World. Some of these sensitivities are discussed in the following paragraphs.

For example, in 1968, according to one scale of comparison (aid as a percentage of gross national product, after allowing for differences in the terms of lending), Sweden was ranked 11th among the 16 members of the Development Assistance Committee (DAC). It ranked low only because it came relatively late into the process of aid-giving. In most of the standard commentaries on aid, Sweden was regarded as being one of the most dynamic (White, 1974, p. 57). But since the mid-1970s (as pointed out in Chapter 3), Sweden has emerged as one of the leading aid-donors in terms of aid given as a percentage of its GNP.

Also, Sweden specifies its aid policy objectives, but only in general terms as support for aid-recipients that deem to adopt especially laudable development postures (as a matter of fact, I was fortunate to attend a development conference at Uppsala during my studies in Sweden in the Fall 1982–the conference, which was sponsored by the Swedes, became a forum for Third World development experts and ministers to discuss how Sweden's aid can better serve the underdeveloped states). Such specifications are used not as a means to interfere into recipients' domestic matters but to possess the latitude in the geographical distribution of its (Sweden) aid. The strategy, although may be open to challenges, is moderately effective in mobilizing some sort of domestic political support for Swedish aid packages (White, 1974, p. 53).

In addition, Sweden had subtly favored aid-recipients such as Vietnam whose policies too obviously did not support Western interests. But the Swedish government had also tempered this approach by not going so far as to offend the susceptibilities of the liberal intellectual, the Christian churches, and useful sources of domestic support for its aid program (White, 1974, p. 75).

Furthermore, Sweden has demonstrated that it can be wedded to the notion of identifying itself with its development projects in the underdeveloped states. The most striking example of such an identification was one of it bilateral loans to India. 'This loan was intended to finance contracts awarded, after competitive bidding, to suppliers in countries which could not be persuaded to subsidize the contract with tied bilateral finance. If such a loan remains unutilized, this can be taken as evidence that it has been effective in strengthening the recipient's bargaining position with sources of tied bilateral aid,' asserted John White (1974, p. 263).

In 1980, when aid from DAC members to Vietnam declined to $151.9 million from a high of $702 million in 1974 (reflecting a decline in Western aid after the liberation of Saigon), the decline would have been greater had Sweden not provided Vietnam with $91.9 million in aid. Also, out of the $35.8 million Angola received in aid from DAC members in 1980, $17 million of that came from Sweden. And Mozambique, which got $114.8 million from DAC members, received $35.8 million of that aid from Sweden. In that same year (1980), Cuba received $11.1 million from DAC, of which $3.8 million came from Sweden (as expected, nothing was provided by Britain and the USA for Cuba) (Hayter and Watson, 1985, pp. 17-19). This clearly shows Sweden's support for states that once opted for non-capitalist approaches to development. In concert with human rights lobbyists within President Jimmy Carter's Administration, the British Labor Government and few other European governments had pushed to block Chile's access to funds from the international financial institutions. And when the United States, for example, sought to stop the World Bank and the IMF from lending funds to certain left-wing governments, Sweden was critical of these institutions' refusal to lend to such governments (Hayter and Watson, 1985, pp. 54-238). Given the preceding disposition, it would be farfetched, therefore, to contend that Sweden's support for the liberation movement in South Africa might have hinged upon expected trade advantages for the Swedes when the white South African regime became obsolete.

Another instrument the Swedish government used to inform its citizenry in order to support its anti-Apartheid policy was the Nordiska Afrikaninstitutet (Scandinavian Institute of African Studies). The Institute was unwavering in its effort to inform Nordic and other citizens about the evils of the white minority regime in South Africa. By 1986, the Institute had published about 70 volumes and sponsored more than 20 lectures dealing with South Africa. The publications included *Amandla! Maatla!: Sydafrika skal Blive Vort*, *The Enemy: The S.A. Apartheid*, *Torture in South Africa* and *Forced Removals in South Africa*. The lectures included Mai Palmberg's 'South Africa to the Functionaries of the Swedish UN Association,' 'South Africa–Civil War,' and Kirsten Holst Petersen's 'Introduction to Black South African Literature' (SIAS, Newsletters, 1983-1986).

The Institute was established in 1962 to promote African studies among Nordic scholars. It is an administrative authority under the Swedish Ministry of Foreign Affairs and governed by a Board of Directors made up of representatives from all the Nordic countries. The Institute's activities are financed principally by the Swedish government (70 per cent), while Denmark, Finland and Norway each contribute 10 per cent of the funding (SIAS, Newsletters).

During the early 1960s, interest in the African continent increased rapidly among the Nordic countries. As the African countries gained their independence, the Nordic countries established cultural, economic and political links with them. The Nordic countries also extended considerable development cooperation with the newly independent states. This led to the establishment of the Scandinavian Institute of African Studies (SIAS, Newsletters).

The Institute was situated in Uppsala due to the longstanding tradition of

African studies at the University of Uppsala–a tradition that in the last four decades has received new vitality through development research. The University Library of Uppsala possesses an extensive collection of African literature, and the theological and humanistic faculties at the University have been engaged in research dealing with Africa for many decades. Since the 1960s, many researchers in the social and natural sciences have also specialized in development issues concerning Africa. In addition, the Swedish University of Agricultural Sciences has increased its activities in development problems in Africa, continuing the tradition of its predecessor, the Agricultural College of Sweden. Furthermore, the Institute collaborates with the Swedish International Development Agency's (SIDA's) Course Center in Uppsala in providing relevant literature and designing and teaching specialized courses for aid workers traveling to Africa (SIAS, Newsletters).

As mandated, the Institute promotes studies on the African continent within the Nordic nations. It encourages and initiates scientific research on and instruction about Africa; it has a documentation center for African research; it disseminates information about current African affairs through courses, lectures and seminars; and it assists in the training of personnel for service in Africa. Within its areas of activities, the Institute also cooperates with other government agencies, non-governmental organizations and individuals in the Nordic states and internationally (SIAS, Newsletters).

The Institute's library is the only one in Scandinavia that specializes in modern Africa. Its key subject areas are modern history, politics, economics, social relationships and education. It also has a comprehensive collection of bibliographies. For its acquisition, it cooperates with The University Library of Uppsala, which is endowed with an extensive and important collection of Africana and continues to acquire literature on Africa's earlier history, ethnography, archaeology and linguistics. The Institute's library has more than 30,000 titles and approximately 600 periodicals of different kinds–newspapers, journals, annuals, as well as African government publications–dealing mainly with development plans, gazettes and statistics. It has a joint catalog covering literature on Africa that is housed in other research libraries in the Nordic countries. Lists of the library's new acquisitions are edited quarterly and collected subsequently into an annual bibliography. The library also produces a list of periodicals that can be obtained free of charge. It is open to the general public. All of its material can be borrowed, with the exception of periodicals, government publications and bibliographies. Its books can also be borrowed through local libraries in the Nordic countries (SIAS, Newsletters).

Every few years, the Institute organizes large international conferences dealing with African issues. Topics covered have included refugee problems, adult education, political boundaries, development of cooperatives, press coverage of news from Africa, multinational corporations operating in Africa, Southern African problems, and Africa's economic situation. African and other international experts are invited to engage in discussions with their Scandinavian colleagues. The Institute also conducts Nordic research seminars to explore special themes. It invites Scandinavian researchers to discuss methodology and theory, empirical evidence, and the relevance of research to development. Most papers presented at seminars and summary of plenary sessions are published as Seminar Proceedings (SIAS, Newsletters).

On a few occasions each month, the Institute convenes afternoon seminars on various topics dealing with development in Africa. The seminars are usually held on Wednesday from 3:00 to 5:00 p.m. in one of the Institute's lecture rooms. Presenters include internationally know Africanists, as well as younger researchers from the Nordic universities. Upon request, the Institute can organize shorter specialized courses on Africa for businessmen, journalists or teachers whose work is linked with the continent (SIAS, Newsletters).

The Institute provides financial support for research on Africa in the Nordic countries. It does this through two types of grants. The first are study grants for students and journalists in the Nordic countries for a month's sojourn in Uppsala. The grants cover travel costs, lodging, and per diem during the stay at the Institute. The deadline for submitting applications for the fall term is May 1st, and for the spring term is November 1st. Application forms can be obtained from the Institute. The second are travel grants for research trips to Africa. These grants contribute to travel costs, board and lodging. They are intended to enable shorter research travels to Africa when grantees can make contact with African research institutions and universities in order to plan research projects or carry out lesser research assignments. These grants are earmarked for researchers in Nordic countries. The application deadline is usually October 1st. Applications for these grants can also be obtained from the Institute (SIAS, Newsletters).

When space is available, the Institute accepts guest researchers or visiting students who, for shorter or longer periods (up to six months), need to make use of the Institute's material. Since the Institute does not have an educational program leading to an academic examination or degree, visiting lecturers cannot be engaged (SIAS, Newsletters). However, this does not mean that visiting lecturers are not often asked questions after their presentations. Receptions after lectures usually provide an opportunity to ask presenters questions.

Swedish Diplomatic Missions in the Front-line States

In their examination of diplomacy, Theodore Couloumbis and James Wolfe (1978, p. 115) noted that one of the world's most ancient arts is diplomacy. They alleged that, in a sense, angels were the first diplomats because they carried the messages of God to people. But that it was not until the 14th Century when independent city-states were established in Italy that the persistent examples of resident embassies emerged.

The study of diplomatic missions has, therefore, become important because their functions have become vital in international relations. Roberto Regala, for example, suggested three key functions of diplomatic missions. These are (1) Representation–this task is performed not only by regular diplomatic agents but also by special representatives for a particular mission; (2) Negotiation–this involves engaging in discourse with the aim of reaching an agreement on certain problems that may arise; and (3) Diplomatic Protection–that is, to protect the home state's interests abroad, particularly its citizens (Regala, 1959, pp. 41-55). Martin Mayer, in his *The Diplomats*, delineated two other key functions of diplomatic missions. These include (1) Informing–here, a diplomatic mission is a system that specializes in gathering and analyzing information that would otherwise not be available or comprehensible at the home country's foreign ministry without assistance; and (2) Persuading–that is, diplomatic missions try to sell their countries' positions and products in order to improve the hosts' attitudes toward their governments (Meyer, 1983, pp. 62-91).

However, Mayer also noted that there are cases when diplomats from big states to little ones may act as viceroys in communicating their governments' instructions to host governments that are willing (and sometimes eager) to take orders. As he emphasized,

> In nations as sophisticated and rich as Japan and Italy, and through much of Latin America, the US Ambassador will have an influence in domestic policies: like it or not, he is part of the consensus process, and failure to secure his consent can doom governmental initiatives. To heads of states in East Germany, Czechoslovakia, Mongolia, Afghanistan and Bulgaria, among others, the Soviet ambassador speaks as their master's voice (Meyer, 1983, p. 62).

Thus, in performing their duties, diplomatic missions embrace a wide range of activities in areas such as power politics, economic forces, and the clash of ideologies. Regala, therefore, asserted that diplomacy 'is one of the few professions of the world within whose orbit comes every branch of human activity' (Regala, 1959, p. 24).

But one thing that is vividly apparent in diplomacy is the fact that the majority of the countries in the world tend to establish diplomatic missions in countries they perceive as being vital than others. For example, there are many more embassies in the United States than there are in Malawi. The establishment of embassies in the perceived vital states is, however, not limited to the industrialized countries alone. Even newly independent states are not immune from the practice. As Peter Boyce observed, newly independent states tend to concentrate their diplomatic missions in those states that they perceive to reap more glamor and prestige. The author also delineated a clear pattern that underlie the rationale of early representation for these newly independent states:

Except in the experience of a few minuscule entities, chiefly Samoa, Tonga, Nauru, and the Maldives, commitments have been undertaken early by the government to open missions (1) in the metropolitan capital, which usually means London or Paris, (2) at the United Nations, sometimes with dual accreditation to the United States, and (3) in the capital of a more significant neighboring state... Those with the resources and resolve to open additional missions will normally seek representation in Washington and it not inflexibly committed to the Western ideological camp, to Moscow and Peking as well (Boyce, 1977, p. 145).

However, Sweden's approach to the establishment of diplomatic missions differs not only from those of new states, but those of some developed states as well. As Zara Steiner's survey on foreign ministries around the world revealed, Sweden's diplomatic missions abroad redoubled in thirty years: from 53 in 1947 to 115 in 1981. These missions employed some 1,400 staff members, most of whom were stationed in Europe and North America. But in later years, Sweden established many missions in Africa and Asia (Steiner, 1982, p. 469). Among these are the missions established in the front-line states as they became independent.

In addition to its own diplomatic responsibilities in other states, Sweden has on numerous occasions been favored to serve as a protecting state (that is, nominated by a third party to protect its interests when that state breaches its diplomatic relations with the host State) due to the high incidence of ruptures in the 1970s (Boyce, 1977, p. 163). As some of the front-line states gained their independence, Sweden did not only establish diplomatic missions in them, it also provided them with development aid and increased its aid to the liberation forces. Moreover, as shown in the following section, Sweden's anti-Apartheid vote at the UNGA was quite impressive compared to those of many other Western/Capitalist nations (Bangura, 1987, pp. 187-188).

Sweden's Anti-Apartheid Votes at the United Nations General Assembly

The aims and principles of the UN were set forth in the Organization's Charter in 1945. They are as follows:

1. to maintain international peace and security;

2. to develop friendly relations among nations;

3. to achieve international cooperation in solving international economic, social, cultural and humanitarian problems, and in promoting respect for human rights and fundamental freedoms for all; and

4. to be a center for harmonizing the actions of nations in attaining these common ends (UN, 1981, p. 3).

However, when these principles were being concocted, Sweden, like many other nations, was left out of the process. And quite appropriately, as the Swedish Institute of International Affairs has noted, Sweden was disappointed because it was not invited to become one of the founding members of the new international body–the UN. The Swedish Foreign Minister at the time, Christian Gunther, in his speech shortly before Adolf Hitler committed suicide, expressed the sentiment of his government. He suggested that it was difficult not to notice that the choice of the states that met in San Francisco was not in accordance with the will and power of all concerned states. Gunther specifically stated that 'This is hardly a promising start. After all, this should be a question of laying the foundation stone of a building that weather tempests, not of finding a formula to solve the temporary difficulties of the great powers' (SIIA, 1956, p. 23).

Nonetheless, the fact that Sweden was not invited to the drafting of the Charter did not spur a great debate in the country. This was due to two major reasons. The first was the fact that the press was not enthusiastic about the issue. The second had to do with the fact that the Swedish Parliament deferred debate on the issue to an undetermined future date. In spite of all this, the Swedish government followed the talks in San Francisco with great sympathy, mainly because it appreciated the victorious powers' untiring effort to carry the entire responsibility for the new international organization (SIIA, 1956, p. 23).

And before the Swedish government submitted its application for membership to the UN in 1946, it sought the blessings of the Parliament. Its decision to apply to the new organization was also largely supported by the

Swedish population. The Swedish Institute of International Affairs in June and August 1945, and again in April 1946, conveyed the sentiments of the Swedish people on the issue. In June 1945, 57 per cent of all those interviewed favored Sweden's desire to join the UN; when the question was put to the people for the second time in August, the support declined to 55 per cent of those interviewed; and when the question was once again asked in April 1946, the number of those in favor further declined to 51 per cent (SIIA, 1956, pp. 30-36).

Nevertheless, the ideals of what constitute good international behavior as embodied in the UN Charter have been exemplified by Sweden since it gained membership to the organization. Conor O'Brien testified to this assumption when he observed that Sweden's action in international relations has been independent, disinterested and honorable. Swedes do not spend much time in proclaiming lofty moral principles but would act as men and women would do who were in fact propelled by such principles. Their voting record has been more eloquent than their speech. The record contains few votes against conscience or expediency–'not to offend a neighbor or an ally who happens to be in the wrong–and are then justified at the podium by an anguished access to legal scruple.' Sweden had paid more than its share for all forms of the humanitarian and peace keeping efforts of the UN. It has sent out soldiers and civil servants to pursue some of the dangerous tasks of the organization, and it has been willing to pay the price for peace as evidenced by the death of Folke Bernadotte (1895-1948), Count of Wisborg and later a Swedish diplomat who became famous for his work in exchanging World War II prisoners. He served in the Swedish Red Cross for many years and became its president in 1946. He was shot in May 1948 in the Israeli held territory of Jerusalem after completing his proposals for a permanent peace in Palestine, while acting as a UN-appointed mediator between the Arabs and the Jews). In addition to Bernadotte, Sweden gave the world Dag Hammarskjold who, in turn, gave the UN a focus of moral authority that affected international loyalty in the pursuit of global peace and justice (O'Brien, 1962, pp. 14-15).

While the UN is not charged with the duties of a government or a supra-state to intervene in the internal affairs of any country, 'except when it is acting (through the Security Council) to maintain or restore international peace' (UN, 1981, pp. 3-4), it has been used as an arena to condemn and to propose actions against belligerent states. And, as stated in Chapter 1, South Africa, especially its Apartheid system, became a key issue before the UN since 1946. The UNGA began dealing with the policies of racial discrimination in South Africa in 1946 and South Africa's policies of Apartheid in 1952 (UN, 1981, p. 29). From the very start of these discussions, Sweden played a significant role in the

General Assembly.

When the discussion on the treatment of persons of Indian origin in South Africa began at the UNGA, Sweden proposed a draft resolution suggesting that the question should be addressed through the instrumentality of the International Court of Justice (ICJ). However, the Swedish proposal was rejected by the General Assembly on the ground that the issue was purely a domestic question. And when the question came up again in 1950, the Swedish representative at the time, Sven Grafstrom, made known his regrets about the assembly's early failure to allow the ICJ to make legal opinions on the issue. In light of the situation at the time, Grafstrom suggested that direct negotiations were the best way of solving the problem. Bolivia, Brazil, Denmark, Norway and Sweden then put forward a draft resolution on Sweden's proposal. But when it came to the floor for a vote, Sweden abstained because it felt that the resolution had been modified by amendments which it could no longer support (SIIA, 1956, pp. 190-191).

Besides presenting resolutions, Sweden, as pointed out throughout this book, effectively used the UN as a forum to render its scathing criticism of the Apartheid system. But in spite of this criticism, it is obvious that a nation's true support or non-support for a given issue can be ferreted out by examining its voting record at the UN. And as Hayward Alker, Jr. and Bruce Russett correctly submitted, 'The Assembly has several advantages as a subject of study: its comprehensive membership, agenda, records, and frequent roll-call votes. These votes may occur any time at the request of any member, and record the different national foreign policy positions with unparalleled completeness' (Alker, Jr. and Russett, 1965, p. 19).

Indeed, Sweden's anti-Apartheid voting record was quite impressive when compared to some Western states. Unlike the *Time* magazine's chart (see Table 5.2), the picture on Sweden's anti-Apartheid stance was much differentiated from that of the United States when the voting records of both countries are examined over time (Bangura, 1987, p. 193).

By scanning the preceding chart, one maybe tempted to conclude that the anti-Apartheid stances of Sweden, the United States, Australia and Canada were equal in strength. But when one examines the voting records of some of these countries on UNGA's anti-Apartheid resolutions, one comes up with an entirely different picture. Besides the USSR, which had an average of 100 per cent anti-Apartheid votes, Sweden had a superior anti-Apartheid voting record (an average or 67 per cent) compared to that of the United States (an average of 23 per cent), that of France (an average of 19 per cent), that of Canada (an average of 46 per cent) and that of Italy (an average of 45 per cent) from 1960 to 1984 (see Bangura, 1987, pp. 194-195).

Table 5.2 'BUILDING A WALL: Sanctions or embargoes taken against South Africa'

	A	B	C	D	E	F	G	H	I
USA	X	X	X	X	X	X	X		
Australia	X	X	X	X	X	X	X		
Brazil	X	X					X		
Britain	X	X		X	X	X	X		
Canada	X	X	X	X	X	X	X		
Denmark	X	X	X	X	X	X	X	X	X
France	X	X	X						
Israel	X								
Italy	X	X				X	X		
Japan	X	X	X		X	X	X		X
The Netherlands	X	X	X			X	X		X
Sweden	X	X	X	X	X	X	X		
Switzerland	X	X				X	X		
W. Germany	X								

A is Sale of Arms, B is Sports or Cultural Activities, C is New Investments by Public Enterprises, D is Imports of Krugerrands, E is Government Loans, F is Oil Sales, G is Trade on Selected Terms, H is All Trade, and I is Diplomatic Relations.

Data Source: *Time* magazine, July 7, 1986, p. 33 (Chart by Joe Lertola).

As this chapter shows, laws and norms form the structure of freedom and barriers in Swedish society. However, this structure is far from being rigid. Laws, if formal and written, can be changed. Laws can also be disregarded, or they may produce unlawful actions that are not expected or desired by lawmakers. Norms differ between groups, and they change over time. Laws and norms do interact, albeit not always in a smooth way. Some groups are better at making laws of their norms than others. Swedish political culture has often been described as a rather secluded play of compromises between politicians, generally for the well-being of the people, but not making voters involved directly in decision-making.

All this means that these seemingly external factors could to some extent be regarded as internal, especially in a large polity with important decision-makers. In spite of this flexibility, some laws are clearly fundamental–in the proper sense of the word–to the Swedish society. There is no absolute authority in the sense of unrestricted freedom. Furthermore, the mosaic has several layers–one of which is the ownership of the means of production, another is the political-administrative decision territory, etc.

Chapter 6

The Assassination of Olof Palme

We had come to know him (Olof Palme) not only as a leader of the Swedish people and an international statesman, but also as one of us, a fellow combatant who has made an inestimable contribution to the struggle for the liberation of South Africa....

From Vietnam to Nicaragua, from El Salvador to Palestine, from Sahara to South Africa, across the face of the globe, the flags hang limp and half mast in loving memory of this giant of justice who had become to a citizen of the world, a brother and a comrade to all who are downtrodden.

> –Oliver Tambo's statement of condolence on the assassination of
> Palme (Reddy 1989, p. 1).

Sven Olof Joachim Palme, born on January 30, 1927, was assassinated on February 28, 1986 on a Stockholm street while heading home from a movie theater with his wife, Lisbet. A man in an overcoat approached the couple from behind, drew a Smith and Wesson revolver and shot the prime minister in his back (http://www.wikipedia.org, http://www.karisable.com).

While there are many theories about who could have been behind the murder, reports on the Apartheid regime's connection have been the most substantiated. But to this day, the identity of the culprit remains a mystery.

Recapitulation of the Assassination and Early Investigation

Olof Palme was killed around 11:20 p.m. along Sveavähen. He had dismissed the bodyguards from the security police (SÄPO) that normally protected him. Several eyewitnesses saw a man running away from Palme and his wife, Lisbet, after they heard the shot. Two suspects, known Palme haters, were found to have been acting in unusual ways in the area before and after the shot was fired. One was arrested eight days later, the other three years later. Some men with walkie-talkies and some policemen were observed acting strangely and heard making suspicious comments in the area before the assassination. These events were explained as ongoing secret police operations and classified under the cloak of 'national security.' Shortly after the killing, some policemen and SÄPO agents, known right-wingers or fascists, were seen having a meeting, during which they made Nazi salutes and toasted with champagne the death of Palme, even before the killing was publicized. A former policeman turned weapons dealer lived in an apartment along the killer's escape route. Palme had planned to visit Moscow for a top-level meeting just a month before his assassination. A reward of 50 million Swedish Kronor (US $5 million) was offered for information leading to the arrest and conviction of the killer. But to this day, the weapon has not been found (http://skog.de/epalme1.htm).

The early police investigation was a disaster. The investigation was headed by Stockholm County Police Commissioner Hans Holmér, administrator, Social Democrat, known power player with no police work experience. His bodyguard belonged to the ultra-fascist faction and was convicted for murder and dismemberment. The prosecutors and top security officials on the case were either incompetent or were cowardly career bureaucrats. The most experienced homicide investigators were left out of the investigation or called in too late. As many policemen characterized the early investigation, it was 'a bloody mess' (http://skog.de/enpalme1.htm).

The investigation was soon to involve more than 300 policemen directly plus the rest of the police force indirectly. In later years, the pool of investigators was reduced to 30. The bungling of the investigation inspired the following joke in Sweden: 'The bad news is that the police is after us, the good news is that it is the Swedish police.' Some security police officers were uncooperative, and some evidence and reports were either lost or not given to the investigators (http://skog.de/enpalme1.htm).

Eight days after the assassination, Viktor Gunnarsson, alias Vic Gunnison, was arrested. He was a 33-year-old Swede, fanatic anticommunist, religious, very intelligent, compulsive liar and 'actor' who had spent time in the United States and claimed to have contacts with the Central Intelligence Agency (CIA) and fought in Vietnam. Gunnarsson was arrested twice; and according to Police Inspector Börje Wingren, who was in charge of that part of the investigation, Gunnarsson was the killer. Gunnarsson was seen near the murder site both before and after the killing. His looks and clothes matched some eyewitnesses' descriptions of the man seen running away after the fatal shot and had uttered threatening remarks towards Palme. However,

Gunnarsson was released after the intervention by higher-level police officers maneuvering for position. He later left Sweden for the United States. He was murdered in North Carolina in 1994 a short time after revealing that he was the one described as the killer in Inspector Wingren's book, *He Killed Olof Palme*. According to American police forces, Gunnarsson was either liquidated or killed in a jealousy drama (http://skog.de/enpalme1.htm).

Three years after the killing, Christer Pettersson was arrested. He was a known drug addict and alcoholic who had been convicted several times for violent crimes. Pettersson was identified by, among others, Palme's wife, Lisbet, and fit some eyewitness's descriptions. He was tried and convicted at a lower court in 1989. However, later that year, his conviction was overturned because of procedural mistakes and plenty of conflicting evidence. Among the worst mistakes made during the investigation was allowing Lisbet Palme to set her own rules. She refused to be videotaped during questioning, she was confrontational when told for what to look, and she only allowed certain investigators to interrogate her. Her identification of Pettersson was flawed and later used to acquit him. She was not even called to identify Gunnarsson as the killer. Many investigators still believe that Pettersson killed Palme, since he had no alibi (http://skog.de/enpalme1.htp).

Competing Theories on the Assassination

The murder of Palme gave rise to many theories about who was behind it. They include (1) the Palme family; (2) the Swedish police; (3) the Kurdistan Workers' Party or PKK; (4) the Kroat facist group known as Ustasja; (5) the World Anticommunist League (WACL); (6) Iranian or Iraqi agents; (7) Swedish weapons exporter Bofors; (8) the East German Red Army; (9) the Soviet Union's KGB; (10) Abu Nidal's Palestinian terrorist organization;(11) the Israeli Mossad; (12) the United States CIA, British MI6 and Propagande Due (P2) collaboration; and (13) the Apartheid regime's secret police known as BOSS. Many of these theories are either untenable or lack evidence; a few make more sense, as witnesses have identified individuals suspected of having links with some of these organizations staying in Stockholm during the time of the murder. Of all these theories, the South African connection seems to be the strongest. Thus, the following discussion looks briefly at some of the other theories for which information exist and examines the South African connection in more depth.

The Palme family theory suggested that Palme arranged his own killing or that his wife, Lisbet, and son were behind it. A few claimed that Palme was mentally insane or a heavy user of cocaine, based on excerpts from alleged comments. These claims are farfetched, since the rest of the administration would have noticed such behavior (http://skog.de/enpalme1.htm).

The Swedish police theory proffered the notion that fascist elements in the country's police force were behind the assassination. More than 30 witnesses gave evidence that before and around the time of the murder they saw people, later identified as off-duty policemen or other known persons, talking into walkie-talkies along the Palme couple's route from the movie theater or along the killer's escape route. The inference is that Palme and his wife were kept under surveillance and stalked by a small organized group. Comments overheard by the witnesses indicate that the Palmes were the subject of the discussion. All the policemen identified were known right-wingers, fascists and Palme haters (http://skog.de/enpalme1.htm).

The PKK theory was that the organization was behind the assassination because Palme had declared the group a terrorist organization and many of its members in Sweden were under surveillance (http://archives.tcm.ie). While the PKK's leader, Abdullah Ocalan, was on trial in Turkey in April 2001, a team of Swedish investigators was sent to his prison to interview him about his earlier comments on Palme's assassination. Ocalan denied that his organization had any connection to the murder. Instead, he suggested that a break-away faction from his group, led by his ex-wife, killed Palme to discredit the PKK. Some time after Palme's killing, a number of Kurds living in Sweden were taken into custody; they were released without charge (http://news.bbc.co.uk).

The United States CIA, British MI6 and Propagande Due (P2) collaboration theory hinged on the idea that former American President George Bush and former British Prime Minister Margaret Thatcher wanted Palme eliminated because his (Palme's) actions were contrary to their policy orientation of global domination (Andromidas 1997, p.1). It was reported that three days before the killing, a wire was sent from Licio Gelli, grand master of the Italian freemason lodge, or P2, to Philip Guarino, a close confidant to George Bush, with the following text: "Tell our friend that the Swedish tree will be felled." P2 has been linked to terrorist bombings, kidnaping and murder. It was also reported that a tip of South African-Swedish police collaboration came from the director of the Swedish civil defense organization and claimed that an Englishman known to him had received the information from Britain's MI6. The tape of this information was reported missing. It was further reported that American politician Alan Cranston made known that he received a letter from a prisoner in California with allegations that the WACL had planned the murder. The letter was reported to have disappeared en route to the Swedish embassy in Washington, DC. To this day, these claims remain unsubstantiated (http://skog.de/enpalme2.htm).

Nonetheless, those who purported the CIA-MI6-P2 connection theory pointed out that the CIA had the funds needed, had the experience needed, and in cooperation with Operations Sub-Group would easily have been able to set up the assassination. They argued that the CIA also had very good knowledge on how to manipulate people and had access to drugs that could have been used to prepare or brainwash Gunnarsson to carry out the killing. Moreover, they believed that the CIA would do whatever Bush demanded without question. They also pointed out that around that time, George Bush and former President Ronald Reagan were involved in the Iran-Contra affair (which also had South African ties), which could have been compromised by Palme's attempts to stop the dirty weapons deals. In addition, they believed that due to their fanatical anti-communist stance, Bush and Reagan did not like Palme's attempts to form closer ties with the Soviets; and that since the 1970s, Palme had become a marked man to the United States because of his demonstrations against America's war in Vietnam (http://skog.de/enpalme2.htm).

As stated earlier, reports on the South African connection have been the most substantiated. To understand why the Apartheid regime would regard Palme a staunch enemy and possibly mark him for elimination, it would be helpful to begin with a brief examination of his anti-Apartheid activities.

Palme's Anti-Apartheid Activities

The following recollections by E. S. Reddy, former head of the United Nations Center Against Apartheid, capture the essence of Palme's commitment to abolish Apartheid and to champion the causes of the downtrodden anywhere in the world. In a generation when the response of Western governments to the revolution against colonial and racist domination in Southern Africa was characterized by equivocation and hypocrisy, Palme was one Western leader who consistently and effectively demonstrated his solidarity with the oppressed people, both in words and in action. Under his leadership, Sweden provided generous assistance to the victims of repression and their liberation movements, and to the newly independent states which suffered enormously because of their geographic location and their refusal to betray Africa. Sweden led the way in the West in evoking sanctions against oppressive regimes, thereby reinforcing the faith of Africans in non-racialism and countering moves to complicate their just struggle by making the region a theater of East-West confrontation (Reddy, 1989, p. 1).

Palme was tireless in his efforts to promote international action against Apartheid, especially in the aftermath of the Soweto massacre of 1976 and in the critical period of the 1980s. He was instrumental in obtaining a firm commitment from the Socialist International to support the African liberation struggle, and he constantly challenged the major Western nations that continued to obstruct international action. He was always abreast of the developments in Southern Africa and the views of the leaders of liberation movements whom he met frequently. He was never paternalistic and constantly emphasized that Africans must be helped in the context of their own choices. He always pointed to the fundamental moral issues: the suffering of the people, their aspirations and their legitimate rights. His commitment was total, and he was always anxious to educate the people first to obtain their support (Reddy, 1989, p. 1).

Palme's contribution to justice, human rights and peace was the result of his unwavering commitment to human solidarity since his early youth. At the age of 19, he joined other Swedish students in donating blood to raise funds for scholarships to South African students. His feeling of solidarity was strengthened by his year's study in 1948 in the United States, where he saw the evil of racism, and by his travel to India and other Asian countries in 1953 as leader of the Swedish student movement. Soon after the Sharpeville massacre of 1960, as a member of the Swedish International Development Authority (SIDA), Palme assisted in providing a government grant to the Nordic student movements to set up a scholarship program for South African refugees. As a member of the Cabinet from 1963, he participated in decisions which placed Sweden in the forefront of Western countries in action against Apartheid and in support of African liberation movements. No matter his portfolio, he always spoke against Apartheid and for international action against colonialism and racism (Reddy, 1989, p. 2).

In 1965, Sweden became the first Western nation to advocate binding sanctions by the United Nations against South Africa. That same year, Sweden made its first contribution to the Defense and Aid Fund and other agencies for humanitarian assistance to political prisoners in South Africa and their families. The following year, when the Defense and Aid Fund was banned in South Africa, Sweden gave the organization confidential grants. Sweden also became a major contributor to the United Nations and other funds for humanitarian assistance to the victims of Apartheid and for scholarships for young South Africans, contributing many times its share under any criteria. In March of 1966, Palme chaired the International Conference on South West Africa that was organized by the British Anti-Apartheid Movement in Oxford. This conference not only drew attention to the brutal oppression in the territory, it also helped to crystalize opinion in favor of ending South Africa's mandate to administer the territory. After the International Court of Justice (ICJ) disappointed hopes of a judicial remedy by its abortive verdict of July 1966, the UNGA terminated the mandate by an overwhelming vote on October 27, 1966 (Reddy, 1989, p. 2).

In April of 1966, Oliver Tambo visited Stockholm at the invitation of the Social Democratic Party. Palme invited him to his home to celebrate the coming of spring with his family on April 30, 1966, in a gesture of recognition of the liberation movement, and marched with him in the May Day parade the next day. This began a close friendship between the two men. In subsequent years, Palme established close personal relationships with leaders of other Southern African liberation movements. When Palme became Prime Minister in 1969, the situation in Southern Africa was cause for serious concern. The white minority in Southern Rhodesia (now Zimbabwe) had declared unilateral independence and South African forces had moved into that country in open defiance of the colonial power, the United Kingdom. Wars between colonial and racist authorities and liberation movements were taking place in Angola, Mozambique, Namibia and Rhodesia. The repression of Africans increased. The 'unholy alliance' of the minority regimes in Rhodesia and South Africa, and the Portuguese fascist regime, posed a challenge to the international community. Yet, there was little international action. The liberation movements and their friends had to make persistent diplomatic and political efforts, including especially the mobilization of the public in the Western countries, to get even slight progress in international action. Again Sweden, together with other Scandinavian countries, was the most responsive to appeals from Africa and the United nations, and Palme was a major architect (Reddy, 1989, p. 2).

The liberation movements required greater assistance, as their needs greatly increased with the launching of armed struggles and the establishment of liberated areas in Angola, Guinea-Bissau and Mozambique. They were able to get assistance, however, only from the Communist countries, mainly in kind, and modest amounts from poor non-aligned countries and public organizations in the West. This situation led the Swedish government to give direct assistance to African liberation movements, and it was the only Western government to do so for several years. It increased the assistance year-by-year; and by 1986, it had contributed well over 700 million Kronor to the liberation movements in Southern Africa and the victims of oppression (Reddy, 1989, p. 2).

Meanwhile, progress on sanctions against South Africa proved to be difficult. While several smaller Western nations had followed the Swedish lead by supporting proposals for sanctions in the United Nations, it was impossible to get a binding resolution from the Security Council because of the vetoes or threats of vetoes by Britain, France and the United States. Sweden and other smaller countries felt that sanctions must be binding and global to be effective, and that action by them alone would be futile. That meant no action at all, even by Sweden, except for discouraging Swedish businesses from making new investments in South Africa. After the Soweto massacre, however, Sweden and Norway led the Western states by taking national action to stop investments in South Africa and pressing for binding measures in the United Nations. Palme and the Social Democrats, then as the opposition party, proposed in the Riksdag the prohibition of new investments in South Africa and initiatives in the United Nations to promote such action by all countries. Administrative action was taken immediately, and legislation prohibiting new investments was adopted in 1979. This marked the beginning of a series of actions by Sweden, including ending air links with South Africa, stopping of visa-free entry to South Africans, supporting boycotts of South Africa in sports and other cultural activities, extending the investment ban to include transfer of technology, and banning virtually all trade with South Africa (Reddy, 1989, pp. 2-3).

Palme was outraged by the continuing violence against schoolchildren in South Africa after the Soweto massacre, the attacks by the racist regimes against neighboring states, and the hypocrisy of the major Western states in condemning Apartheid while continuing even military cooperation with the Pretoria regime. He was also gravely concerned over the possibility of military confrontation between the superpowers (the United States and the Soviet Union) in Southern Africa. Beginning in 1976, Palme played a key role by devoting a great deal of effort to promote action by the Western world, especially by the Socialist movement, to support the oppressed people in Southern Africa. He rejected the criticism of liberation movements for resorting to armed struggle. He warned people in the West not to moralize against those who were forced, by the intransigence and escalating brutality of the oppressors, to resort to violent resistance. He pointed out that the cooperation of Western governments with the racist regimes in Southern Africa helped to fuel the situation. He denounced moves by major Western states to give assurances to the Apartheid regime in return for its cooperation in facilitating negotiated settlements in Namibia and Rhodesia. He pointed out that the Apartheid regime would cooperate only if there were sanctions and pressure, and that the impediment to peace in the Southern African region was Apartheid itself. He stressed that lack of action by the United Nations should not serve as an alibi for passivity as regards to taking action at the national level. He proposed a program of action that would (a) end all military cooperation with racist regimes; (b) pressure the major Western states to support binding sanctions by the United Nations; (c) implement unilateral measures, pending such binding sanctions, especially to end investments in South Africa and stop loans to that country; (d) support liberation movements and the oppressed people; (e) assist the independent states in Southern Africa; and (f) encourage action by churches, trade unions and other non-governmental organizations to support the liberation of the region. He became a sponsor of the World Campaign against Military and Nuclear Cooperation with South Africa (WCMNCSA), initiated by an ANC leader, Abdul S. Minty, to ensure the full implementation and strengthening of the United Nations arms embargo against South Africa. He constantly stressed that Social Democrats should identify themselves with the struggle against oppression. The Social Democratic movement, Palme pointed out, had arisen as a liberation movement of people denied political and human rights. He added that the movement should be the voice of workers and other people oppressed through history, and that the Social Democratic parties in Europe must be linked by solidarity with the oppressed of Africa. As he put it at the Socialist International Congress held in Geneva in 1976,

> Democratic socialists should never stand on the side of colonialism and racialism. In each individual instance we must stand on the side of the poor and oppressed peoples and give our support to the continued struggle for liberation in Southern Africa....It is not only a question of contacts and dialogue but of identifying ourselves with the liberation struggle of the oppressed majority of this planet (Reddy, 1989, pp. 3-4).

By the time Palme returned to power in 1982, Zimbabwe had gained its independence. However, the Apartheid regime was increasing its attacks against neighboring states and repression against the rising resistance in Namibia and South Africa. The Apartheid regime was emboldened by the policy of 'constructive engagement' pursued by the Reagan administration and' the stubborn opposition by the conservative governments in Britain and West Germany to any sanctions against it. A critical situation arose in 1984 when Mozambique, due to devastation from South African aggression and destabilization, signed the Nkomati accord with South Africa. It appeared that the front-line states were weakening just when resistance in South Africa was on the rise. Encouraged by some Western powers, the Pretoria regime sought to break through its isolation and assert suzerainty over the whole of Southern Africa (Reddy, 1989, p. 4).

Palme recognized the need to provide greater political and material support to the front-line states and to find ways to support the resistance movements inside South Africa, especially the United Democratic Front (UDF) and the independent trade unions. Sweden rapidly increased its assistance to the front-line states, amounting to more than $300 million in 1986. It became the major source of support to the movements struggling against Apartheid inside South Africa in the face of brutal repression. The meeting of the Foreign Ministers of the Nordic and front-line states, which Sweden organized in June 1984, and the meeting in September of the Socialist International with the front-line states and liberation movements, of which Palme was the major architect, contributed greatly to protecting and advancing the resistance to the Apartheid regime's aggression and repression. At the same time, the Swedish government increased its national sanctions against South Africa and took initiatives to strengthen the Nordic program of action against Apartheid. Sweden worked closely with Non-aligned states to push for stronger United Nations action in response to the upsurge of resistance in South Africa from 1984 and the imposition of a state of emergency in the country. Until his assassination, Palme continued to promote action for the emancipation of Africa. His last major address was to the Swedish People's Parliament against Apartheid, a week before he was murdered. He concluded his speech with the clarion call that 'We must live up to our responsibility for bringing the repulsive system (i.e. Apartheid) to an end' (Reddy, 1989, p. 4).

The South African Connection

The following sample of Swedish press comments on the allegations made by former South African security agent Dirk Coetzee that Apartheid South Africa was behind the assassination of Olof Palme, as summarized by Nidia Hagström and Sarah Roxström on September 30, 1996, seem to capture the sentiments of the Swedish people on the issue:

1. The morning liberal daily *Uppsala Nya Tidning* points out that Palme's murder and the failure to find his killer amount to a national trauma, adding that the information now coming from South Africa is truly sensational. This may well turn out to be yet another dead end in the hunt for the murderer, but Coetzee's statements deserve a thorough investigation.

2. The Conservative newspaper *Smålandsposten* agrees. This theory is

not less likely than many others which have floated around since the shooting, even if it seems far-fetched to believe that former prime minister Olof Palme's support for the ANC and active involvement in the struggle against apartheid are the motive for the assassination, says the newspaper.

3. Center party daily *Länsindning i Södertälje* wonders why the South African connection has not been carefully checked as the one attributing the murder to the Kurdish labor party once upon a time. And this newspaper suggests that a future investigation should be carried out by a completely different team of detectives. This way one could avoid the risk of prestige getting in the way of a thorough job. Another center-party newspaper, *Skånska Dagbladet*, follows the same line of reasoning, renewing a suggestion once made by one of Palme's sons: that foreign investigators, possibly from another Nordic country, be assigned the task.

4. Liberal daily *Vestmanlands läns tidning* rounds off by warning against a potential pitfall: the fact that a South African connection would be such an 'attractive' solution to a murder that shook the whole Swedish nation. It wold mean that some shady figure working for Pretoria's racist regime would have killed Palme because of Sweden's support for South Africa's oppressed black population. This would be a lot more comforting than the alternative of a single, confused Swede who just happened to shoot his own prime minister (http://www.lyastor.liu.se).

In September of 1996, the former chief of a covert South African police hit squad, Eugene de Kock, stated that an Apartheid spy was involved in the assassination of Olof Palme. De Kock made the allegation while testifying in a mitigation of sentence hearing before a judge who had convicted him in August of that year of six murders and a series of other crimes. De Kock added that the murder was carried out under Craig Williamson's Operation Long Reach, and that it should be investigated before it was covered up. Williamson was one of the Apartheid regime's most effective spies during the 1970s and 1980s and had admitted to carrying out bombings and other actions against anti-Apartheid activists. De Kock had confessed during the trial that he and Williamson collaborated in blowing up the ANC offices in London. He concluded by stating that he had the police station cells keys made and could have escaped from custody, but that he had chosen to face the charges against him. He had also applied to the country's Truth and Reconciliation Commission for amnesty for his crimes. The Commission, set up to heal the wounds of Apartheid, was given powers to grant amnesty to perpetrators of human rights abuses and crimes against humanity who confess to their deeds (Ndabazandile, 1996, pp. 1-2). However, in October of 1996, Williamson emphatically denied that he had anything to do with the killing of Palme, and that he did not know who was involved (Hanna, 1996, p.2).

Speaking at a media briefing at his attorney's office in Rosebank, Johannesburg, Williamson sated that although Palme was not considered 'a friend' by the Apartheid regime, he was opposed to Soviet-style Marxism and was, therefore, not perceived as a threat to South Africa. His lawyer, Levin, revealed that he and Williamson had met Glen Goosen, head of the Truth and Reconciliation Commission's investigating unit, and that it was possible Williamson would make a submission to the commission (http://www.anc.org. za).

Williamson had arrived in South Africa after being freed from a Luanda, Angola jail. He was arrested by Angolan authorities who initially said he was picked up in the "Cancer Two" clean-up program designed to rid Angola of illegal aliens. While in detention in Angola, Williamson was questioned by Swedish investigators, led by Jan Danielsson, and South African secret service officials regarding the allegations by De Kock that he (Williamson) was involved in the murder of Palme. Levin questioned the legality of the questioning in terms of international protocols, as Williams did not received legal representation, and promised to send a letter of protest to the Swedish government. Asked why he agreed to the investigation, Williamson responded that 'The circumstances prevailing at the time made cooperation rather attractive' (http://www.anc.org.za).

Roger Ballard-Tremeer, South Africa's ambassador to Angola, confirmed that 40 South Africans were arrested in "Cancer Two." However, he was not aware whether other South Africans were still in jail or of any new arrests. Levin stated that since Williamson was not deported from Angola, he was welcome to return there and continue his business whenever he wished. Williamson reported that he had been doing legitimate business in Angola, importing fresh produce, consumer goods and working in mining contracting, and had a valid work permit. He added that he was told he could not return to South Africa and was refused passage on the chartered flight from Luanda to Johannesburg on which the Swedish investigators and the South Africans left Angola, and that he was not told why. Williamson concluded by stating that he had not been to Sweden since 1980, had never met Palme, and that 'Operation Long Reach'–the operation in which Palme was allegedly assassinated–did not exist until after Palme's death (http://www.anc.org.az).

On January 20, 2003, the Stockholm daily newspaper, *Dagens Nyheter*, reported that a Swedish businessman by the name of Kent Ajland said that a group of South African private investigators had identified a South African agent living outside of the country at the time as Palme's assassin. It was also reported that Ajland stated that he had received documentation from the South African investigators showing that the agent, who was not named on the press report, was in Stockholm on the night Palme was murdered. Furthermore, it was mentioned that Ajland had told another Stockholm newspaper, *Aftonbladet*, that he received a tipoff on the Palme killing from contacts in South Africa during a business trip in the region. It was also reported that Lars Nylen, head of the special Swedish police task-force in charge of the continuing investigation of the Palme case, was cautious in drawing any conclusion from the evidence, saying that no new facts had emerged and no arrests were anticipated (http://iafrica.com).

On January 21, 2003, it was revealed that according to 'an original document' dated November 20, 1985, a copy of which was shown to *Dagens Nyheter*, Palme's assassin was a South African secret agent whose orders came directly from Pieter. W. Botha's chief security advisor, who was not named. The document was said to be a letter sent to Williamson. According to the letter, which referred to the operation by the codename 'Slingshot,' Palme was to be killed between February 21 and 23, 1986 during an anti-Apartheid conference, which was attended by ANC leader Oliver Tambo. The claims were based on research conducted by former high-ranking South African soldiers who acquired their country's military archives and interviewed agents. Their work was financed by Ajland and Tommy Lindström, a former Swedish police chief. A former South African navy officer, Ponnie van Vuurum, was also reported to have told *Dagens Nyheter* that he had no doubt about the identity of the killer. He was quoted as saying the following:

> We have all the evidence, including the documents revealing who gave the orders, the motive, and the perpetrator....The murderer has been on the run for 17 years (...) He has no income, and no job. He is holding a fake passport (http://iafrica.com).

On January 24, 2003, it was reported that according to the foreign affairs department in Pretoria, the Swedish authorities had not contacted the South African government in connection to the latest allegations about the killing of Palme. Meanwhile, the Afrikaans daily *Beeld* reported that a 1985 report of Military Intelligence, as it was known then, stated that Palme should be regarded as an enemy of Apartheid. The newspaper also named a former security policeman to have said that details about him had been leaked to the Swedish media in connection with the murder. The man, however, denied ever having been in Sweden. South African foreign affairs department spokesperson Ronnie Mamoepa stated that 'It has always been a generally held belief that the apartheid agents were responsible for the death...(of Olof Palme).' He added that the 'South African authorities [had] not been contacted by the Swedish authorities concerning the renewed allegations of South African complicity in the assassination of Prime Minister Palme' (http://iafrica.com).

On January 26, 2003, it was confirmed by Swedish authorities that they had received documents that could prove South Africa's involvement in the murder of Olof Palme. A former South African agent was identified as the assassin (http://www.suntimes.co.za).

On January 30, 2003, it was reported that Swedish police had dismissed the theory that Roy Allen, a former secret agent for South Africa's Apartheid regime, was involved in the murder of Palme. Police Chief Nylen was also reported to have confirmed media reports that investigators had traveled abroad to question Allen (who now lives in Australia), who denied that he murdered Palme. Nylen was reported to have concluded that the interrogation had strengthened earlier police theories that reports fingering Allen were an attempt to deceive intelligence services (http://AfricaOnline.com).

So the question that one must ask is why the South African connection to the assassination of Palme has been the most substantiated. The following summary of Klaas de Jonge's investigation of the issue provides some good answers.

According to the journalist-researcher Sven Anér, the African specialist and journalist Per Wästberg told the Swedish police five days after Palme was killed that there could be a South African connection, but the police did not even bother to accept Wästberg's two letters as they were not interested in investigating the South African trail. Anér was convinced that the Swedish police had a direct hand in the assassination of Palme; others did not believe this, albeit nobody denies the possibility of some indirect involvement by the police (Jonge, http://www.totse.com).

A few days after the assassination of Palme, the British Intelligence agency, MI6, received a report stating that the man who had killed Palme had been acting under orders from the South African security police. Members of the death squad Koevoet, or COIN, were said to have carried out the murder and that Williamson designed the plans with the aid of Swedish policemen (Jonge, http://www.totse.com).

At about the same time, Karl-Gunnar Bäck of the Civil Defense Force

Association was contacted by an old acquaintance from England who told him that the MI6 had information on the murder of Palme. The informant claimed that Palme was assassinated by a member of the South African security forces with the assistance of a Swedish policeman. Bäck recorded the information on a cassette and sent it to SÄPO in Uppsala. Months passed by and nobody from the security police force contacted him. It was not until late summer in 1986 that Bäck was informed that 'the leads had been investigated and had led to nothing.' Bäck was surprised that SÄPO had neither bothered to speak to him and had not asked for the informant's name. It was later learnt that the investigators of the Palme case neither knew of the tape nor whether the lead was investigated. SÄPO claimed that it could not find the tape (Jonge, http://www.totse.com).

The investigators of the Palme case received another lead on a South African connection. An informant, a known thug who was serving a jail sentence at the time, said that he was convinced that Swedish policemen helped South African agents to assassinate Palme. Some Swedish policemen were members of the International Police Association (IPA). They ran a training camp in Rydsford and had made several trips to South Africa where they had met that country's security policemen. The policemen and the IPA were said to have had secret premises and weapons at a meeting place in Wallingatan 32, Stockholm, a few bocks from the murder scene. According to an informant, these policemen were Nazis, bore arms while off duty and had frequent contacts with South African agents. It was also reported that the WACL certainly had an office in the same building (Jonge, http://totse.com).

An internal investigation was conducted on six policemen known for their extreme right-wing sympathies and who had paid several visits to South Africa in the mid-1980s (1985-87). The Normalm police precinct where the six worked is next door to the Birger jarl Hotel where Williamson used to stay when he visited Sweden. The policemen of this precinct had a record of police brutality during the 1980s. They had a so-called "baseball league" which was involved in extreme right-wing politics. They also left the precinct open to so-called private security companies involved in arms trade. According to Alcalá, policemen involved in these undemocratic, Nazi and conspiratorial practices were never investigated when reports were made abut them (Jonge, http://totse.com).

The Norrmalm precinct covers the area were Palme was assassinated. Some policemen were patroling the streets the night of the murder, but they claimed not to have seen anything and, according to Anér, the policemen did not react adequately after the murder was reported. One policeman was reported to be too exhausted to chase after Palme's murderer, due to having consumed a can of coke just before arriving at the scene of the crime (Jonge, http://www.totse. com).

Ake Malström, a newspaper photographer, was listening in on a police radio frequency the night of the assassination. He reported to have overheard a conversation between two police officers moments after the shooting. The alleged conversation went as follows: 'It's cold up here,' to which the officer replied, 'It's over now. The prime minister is dead.' Malström filed a statement, but he was never called in for questioning. According to Tor Sellström, Johan Coetzee was sitting next to a lady of the Swedish Embassy in Pretotia during a diplomatic function in early 1996. When Coetzee heard that the lady was from Sweden, he said that he remembered the tough days when Sweden and South Africa did not have good contacts. He added that he as a commissioner of police always had good contacts, and that Swedish police officers had visited South Africa through the IPA. Swedish journalists who visited South Africa and tried to see the guest-books of the IPA in Cape Town, Johannesburg and Pretoria were told that the books had been destroyed (Jonge, http://www.totse. com).

According to Anders Hasselbohm, after Palme was assassinated, Bertil Wedin (alias 'Morgan' and 'John Wilson'), a Swedish right-winger who had in the past worked for Craig Williams, initiated the Kurdish PKK-connection, which soon became the main lead in the Swedish police's search for Palme's murderer. The PKK is the Turkish government's main enemy that has battled Ankara's security forces in Turkey since 1984. Wedin had faked this link and passed it on to a journalist of the Turkish daily *Hurriyet*. Wedin named seven members of the PKK group to have been involved in the assassination. A few months later, Stockholm Police Chief Hans Holmér who was heading the murder investigation stated that the 'PKK was behind the murder of Olof Palme.' Promoted by Holmér and Ebbe Carlsson, this lead prompted the arrest of PKK sympathizers in Sweden. However, later investigators had to abandon the lead (Jonge, http://www.totse.com).

Wedin also was an informant for the Swedish security police. He had openly declared that he was working against the Swedish Social Democratic government and especially against Palme. Wedin was a friend of Göram Assar Oredsson, leader of the neo-Nazi party named Nordiska Rikspartiet. Wedin was an officer of the United Nations peace-keeping forces in the Congo in 1961 and in Cyprus in 1963. In Cyprus, he served as a lieutenant and on the staff intelligence unit in the United Nations forces. When he resigned from the Swedish army in 1966, Wedin went to the American Embassy in Stockholm and demanded that he be sent to Vietnam to fight. He was turned down. In 1967, he became the driving force behind The Committee for a Free Asia–a committee that was planning a counter-tribunal on Vietnam that would investigate 'the murders and atrocities committed by the communist side in the Vietnam war.' At this time, Wedin became a regular informant for SÄPO, providing the agency with information on left-wing Swedes. He also worked for a Swedish bank, Stockholm Enskilda Bank, calling himself a journalist and producing the newsletter *Mediasammandrag* (Media Summary) for the bank. He later confirmed that he was also involved in military intelligence work. In 1976, a Swedish newspaper wrote that Wedin was probably behind newspaper advertisements trying to recruit mercenaries for service in Southern Africa. That same year, he moved with his family to England. He arranged seminars on behalf of Sveriges Industriforbund (Swedish Industries), Svenska Arbetsgivarforeningen (Swedish Employers' Federation) and some 15 other companies, so that Swedish businessmen could meet businessmen, politicians and "thinkers" in Britain (Jonge, http://www. totse.com).

Wedin was recruited to serve as a South African spy by Craig Williamson. The two met in South Africa in 1980. Williamson introduced Wedin to Peter Casselton, based in London, to whom Wedin had to report. Casselton, a British citizen but a South African agent, gave Wedin the codename 'John Wilson.' Wedin became involved in break-ins at various anti-Apartheid organization offices in London. A letter from Williamson to Wedin resulted in a police search of the latter's 12-room house in Townbridge, Kent. The police found stolen material, including notes from documents stolen from the office of the Pan Africanist Congress of Azania (PAC). They also found a map of the area where the PAC office was located, showing the way to the Dollis Hill underground station and sketches of the office itself. Wedin told the police that he was being paid by Williamson 1,000 pounds per month plus costs via a bank account in Switzerland. He also received camera equipment. After being interrogated at the Rochester Row police station in London, Wedin was soon released on bail (Jonge, http://www.totse.com).

Unlike the other two culprits, Casselton and Aspinall, Wedin pleaded not guilty at the court proceedings at the Old Bailey on December 17, 1982. The judge agreed that he could remain free on bail. During his trial in April, Wedin claimed never to have given any information to the South Africans. The judge then noted that he could not understand what Wedin had done to earn the money the South Africans had paid him. Wedin claimed that he had used the money to write a book on Soviet subversive activities; no one has ever seen the book. He admitted that he had been at the PAC office on three occasions to conduct interviews. About the map of the area where the PAC office was located, Wedin claimed that he had a 'bad memory' and needed to find his way. He never had to account for the sketches of the inside of the office.

However, after being acquitted, Wedin admitted to the press that he had supplied information to the Africa Aviation Consultants company on the Isle of Man. But he claimed that he had done it in good faith, having no knowledge that Willaimson and Casselton's company was a front for the South African security service. In South Africa, the Williamson-led operation was touted as a great success (Jonge, http://www.totse.com).

According to Hasselbohm, in 1985, Wedin held a major position in the organization called Victims Against Terrorism (VAT)–a major South African propaganda operation in Europe. In May 1985, VAT staged a demonstration outside the ANC office in London, accusing the organization of carrying out terrorist acts. Later, Arthur Kemp, another South African agent who was a prime suspect in the murder of Chris Hani in 1993, became a leading figure in VAT (Jonge, http://www.totse.com).

In November 1985, Wedin and his family flew to Northern Cyprus. On their disembarkation cards, they declared that they were going to settle there permanently. Wedin was issued a Turk-Cypriot identification card in March of 1986. On at least one previous occasion, Wedin, using the undercover name 'John Wilson,' had, for unknown reasons, gone to Cyprus together with Casselton. Immediately after his arrival in Northern Cyprus, Wedin was employed by the Ministry of Information there. His job included working for Radyo Bayrak, a Turk-Cypriot radio station. He used the radio to fire off vicious attacks against the Social Democrats in general and Palme in particular. Wedin also became the Middle East correspondent for the Swedish ultra-right journal, *Kontra* (Counter-guerilla). It was not until after Palme's assassination that Wedin took on his new role as the initiator of the PKK-connection. He denied any involvement in the assassination of Palme (Jonge, http://www.totse.com).

Heine Hüman is alegedly a Swede of South African origin who went to Sweden in the early 1980s and now lives in Florida, United States. During the time of Palme's murder, Hüman lived in a depressive place outside of Uppsala and worked at a car repair shop. Fourteen minutes after Palme's killing, an elderly couple in Bromma, Stockholm received a mysterious telephone call with the message: 'The job is done, Palme is dead.' With the only difference of one digit in the area code (Stockholm is 08 and Uppsala-area is 018), their number corresponded to the number of a telephone in a room of a clubhouse of which allegedly only Hüman had the key. Hüman left Sweden in a hurry after Palme was assassinated, without saying goodbye to his neighbors. These neighbors, who were interviewed by Swedish news reporters, revealed that there was funny business going on at night at his place. A Swedish journalist tracked down Hüman in Florida where he now lives under another name in a place outside of Miami where a lot of American ex-intelligence people are retired. When interviewed, he denied having any involvement in the assassination of Palme. In the past, Hüman had claimed to be a South African agent and that he had been involved in Dulcie September's murder. ANC intelligence officers interviewed Hüman in Harare, Zimbabwe; but according to Tor Sellström, who lived in Harare during the same time, there were doubts about Hüman's claims. While the officers believed that he might have done something, they also found him to be incoherent (Jonge, http://www. totse.com).

Three men were also reported to have camped out in a white combi (camping van) for some weeks before the murder. It was cold that winter, with snow on the ground; but to avoid registration, the men did not stay in a hotel. The camping van was believed to have come from neighboring Finland to the east and possibly drove via Norway in the West. The men were reported to be South Africans (Jonge, http://www.totse.com).

Some Swedish newspapers also reported that two policemen said that South Africa's super-spy, Craig Williamson, was in Stockholm at the time of the anti-Apartheid conference and was there also on the night of the murder. Through the IPA, Williamson allegedly rented a room under a fictitious name in a guesthouse belonging to the IPA on Kammakargatan 36, just two hundred meters from the spot where Palme was shot. Williamson knew Sweden very well. He had infiltrated Operation Daisy–the Geneva-based and Swedish-funded International University Exchange Fund (IUEF). The fund had 'virtually been run from Palme's office' and one of the key links was Bent Carlsson, who was later killed in the Lockerbie bombing. The IUEF gave scholarships to Africans, especially hundreds of opponents of Apartheid, and Latin American students who had fled right-wing regimes. Williamson became deputy director and trusted assistant of the Swedish IUEF director, Lars Gunnar Eriksson, a friend of Palme. The objective of Williamson and Coetzee's project was to infiltrate the ANC through the IUEF. Eriksson was anti-communist and wanted to support a third force, especially the Black Consciousness Movement, which was what the South Africans liked (Jonge, http://www.totse.com).

From 1977 until he was exposed as a spy in 1980, Williamson visited Stockholm on several occasions. He had the ears of Swedish power-brokers and usually stayed at the Birger Jarl Hotel around the corner from the Swedish International Development Agency (SIDA). At least one of these visits (in April 1978) was kept secret from his usual hosts in the Foreign Ministry. Within walking distance of the Ashton Hotel where Williamson was staying was the ANC office, where there was an unexplained break-in. While nothing was reported missing, the files were found to have been ransacked (Jonge, http://www.totse.com).

During a press conference in Stockholm in 1980, Eriksson revealed that Coetzee had approached him in a hotel in Geneva and asked that he keep Williamson's police identity a secret for another six months, so that Williamson could nestle in closer to the ANC. The revelation shocked Eriksson, forcing him to flee to Sweden. When auditors checked IUEF's books, they discovered serious discrepancies. Williamson had been siphoning funds to build Daisy Farm in the Pretoria region. Daisy Farm was designated as Section A–a special unit of the South African police charged with monitoring anti-Apartheid activists abroad and headed by Williamson. He admitted that Wedin and another Sweden (probably Hüman) were working for him. Williamson also admitted to be responsible for the murders of Ruth First and the wife and daughter of the ANC activist Marius Schoon, but he denied being involved in the Palme assassination (Jonge, http://www.totse.com).

The Swedish People's Parliament Against Apartheid (a conference) was organized by the Swedish anti-Apartheid groups and announced a long time before it was actually held from February 21 to 23, 1986. Among the participants were Oliver Thambo, Thabo Mbeki and Abdul Minty of the ANC, as well as representatives of the United Democratic Party (UDF) and the South-West African People's Organization (SWAPO). South African agents could have been sent to Sweden at the time, and Craig Williamson could have been with them. However, during an interview with Tor Sellström, Williams stated that 'Sweden was badly worked and not well penetrated. So it was very much left to political contacts,' which implies the right-wing groups in Sweden that would include men like Hüman and Wedin. Although security was tight, it would still be easy to keep track of the movements of persons like Tambo, Mbeki, etc., because there were places they certainly had to visit before, during and after the 'Parliament.' These places would include the headquarters of the Social Democratic Party (a place Palme visited regularly), the Ministry of Foreign Affairs, the SIDA building, and places in the center of Stockholm not very far from one another. This is an area with which Williamson was quite familiar (Jonge, http://www.totse.com).

A week before Palme was assassinated, in a meeting where he was reading his prepared speech, according to journalist Madi Gray, 'he gestured and put the manuscript down on the desk in front of him. He raised his head (left his prepared speech) and said: "We are all responsible for apartheid. If the world wants apartheid to end, it could end tomorrow by simply withdrawing support to the apartheid regime." At the time it was such a revolutionary statement, that it took everybody's breath away.' It certainly angered both the Swedish extreme right and the Apartheid regime (Jonge, http://www.totse.com).

During the 'Parliament,' the local network and the hitsquad could have been activated against one or more of the representatives of the ANC, UDF or SWAPO, or even against Palme. For some reason, such a plan was never carried out probably due to the tight security. With the center of Stockholm under surveillance, it could have been known that Palme dismissed his bodyguards and went to the movie theater with his wife. This would give the planners at least two hours to carry out the assassination. With the structure already in place, it was an easy task to carry it out. Many police officers said that the murder was too unprofessionally done to be the work of agents. Police Superintendent Hans Ölvebro added that it was 'improbable that a group could have organized itself so quickly.' But a good way for a professional hit-man to hide his trail is to make an assassination look like an unprofessional job, hiding the people behind it as well (Jonge, http://www.totse.com).

As mentioned earlier, Eugene de Kock named Craig Williamson in his mitigation plea at the Pretoria Supreme Court as the mastermind of the Palme assassination. De Kock believed that Wedin, now living in Kyrenia, in North of Cyprus, was the Murderer. De Kock stated that he learnt about the Apartheid regime's involvement in Palme's assassination during a meeting in 1992 or 1993 with Philip Powell, now an Inkatha Freedom Party (IPF) senator (Jonge, http:// www.totse.com).

Dirk Coetzee said that James Anthony White, also a founding member of Operation Long Reach, pulled the trigger that killed Palme. Williamson's military intelligence front, Long Reach, was reporting to Brigadier 'Tolletjie' Botha. Coetzee first learnt about the South African connection through a former agent in the Long Reach outfit, 'Riaan' Stander, a former low-ranking security policeman. Stander also made the same revelations to a Swedish journalist in 1995. He also said that White was assisted in the assassination by a British spy named Mike Irwin (a British marine who served in Northern Ireland and the Falklands war) who also worked for Long Reach. However, Casselton told the Swedish state television that White had nothing to do with the murder, and that the assassin was a European living in hiding somewhere in the Mediterranean (Jonge, http://www.totse.com).

White was a former Selous Scout and once a ruthless killer for Ian Smith's Rhodesia. White was one of the main killers of the Nyadzonia ZANU-camp in Mozambique in August 1976, where 600-1,000 people perished. He also made two failed attempts to murder Zimbabwean liberation leader Joshua Nkoma in Lusaka, according to a book by his former Selous Scout commander, Ron Reid-Daly. The first involved a car packed with explosives on a route often taken by Nkomo; the second was an attack on Nkomo's house that destroyed the building and killed several people inside, but not Nkomo. White moved to South Africa after Zimbabwe won its independence in 1980. He was known as a 'loner' mercenary with a history of 'selling [his services] to the highest bidder.' As a founding member of Long Reach, he was also involved in contraband operations in the late 1980s and became a member of a poaching and ivory smuggling network that operated in Zimbabwe (Jonge, http://www.totse.com).

White was linked to both the South African and Mozambican security services. He ran a furniture store on the outskirts of Beira in Mozambique. He manufactured exclusive hardwood furniture and doors through a timber concession he obtained from the Mozambican government. Mozambique's Frelimo government sheltered White for many years. He became close to Frelimo during the latter stages of the war against Renamo when he protested loudly against Renamo's attempts to extort money from businesses working in hardwood forests under Renamo control. However, White denied any involvement in the assassination of Palme (Jonge, http://www.totse.com).

Indeed, Sweden, with Palme as its prime minister, provided more than 50 percent of the ANC's civilian budget in the 1980s. It was also one of the countries that pushed the hardest for sanctions against South Africa and the first to carry them out. Thus, it is not farfetched to expect that if the Apartheid regime was not connected to Palme's assassination, it must have definitely had plans to do so. That the Apartheid regime could even anticipate assassinating Palme is testimony to how his moral stance on racism in South Africa made the white Apartheid government very uncomfortable.

For his work to end Apartheid and probably losing his life for it, it is only fitting that South African President Thabo Mbeki awarded the First Class (Gold, 'Supreme Champion') Order of the Companions of O. R. Tambo Medal to Olof Palme posthumously on December 10, 2002. The other two recipients were India's Mohandas Mahatma Gandhi (posthumous) and Kenneth Kaunda, former president of Zambia, where the exiled ANC was based until 1994 (http://www.geocities.com).

Chapter 7

Conclusions

On October 11, 1978, the Swedish Ambassador to the UN at the time, His Excellency Andres I. Thunborg, accepted one of the eight UN's award for Distinguished Service in the Struggle Against Apartheid on behalf of Prime Minister Olof Palme and also delivered the following acceptance speech on Palme's behalf:

> I deeply regret that I am not able to be present at the ceremony today to receive this award. This is a moment of profound pride and happiness in my life that I wish I could have shared with you all and with all my other friends at the United Nations. I feel most sincerely that this is a very special award, which I am honoured to share with some specially noble people.

> I accept this award in humble awareness of the fact that we participate in the struggle against *apartheid* as a compelling matter of human decency and because of our conviction that we all share a responsibility as human beings to fight against a system that is a disgrace to our world society. In this struggle we stand on the side of those who are oppressed, poor and exploited, because we believe that in the fight against a system that is both evil in itself and a threat to peace there is no middle ground. Our most fundamental feelings of human solidarity leave us no alternative.

> But those who should be honoured and praised today are not some few outsiders who receive awards but rather all those innumerable silent victims of *apartheid* in South Africa itself, all those unsung heroes who risked or gave their lives in a brave fight for human dignity, all those who still suffer daily humiliation under a cruel system of discrimination, all those who had to flee their native country in order to save their lives, their health and their sanity. Those who should be remembered and honoured on this solemn occasion are the children who died in the streets of Soweto, the political prisoners who were beaten and tortured to death on the cold floors of the police cells, the squatters at Crossroads who saw their poor homes and few belongings being demolished and shattered, the women and children who were forced to leave their husbands and fathers to live in material and emotional misery on bantustans far away.

They are, all of them, the real heroes in the fight against *apartheid*. They are in the very front line in this struggle, and the liberation from *apartheid* will be their work and their victory. But they need support, and we should be prepared to give that support whole-heartedly.

The awards that have been bestowed upon us today should be regarded as a solemn expression of our untiring will to contribute to the elimination and eradication of an evil system. These medals should be seen as shining symbols of our hope that one day freedom, justice and peace will triumph in South Africa also (UN Center Against Apartheid, 1978, pp. 22-23).

Indeed, Olof Palme and his fellow Swedish citizens' sentiment on and role in the struggle to eliminate the Apartheid system are captured quite well in the preceding text, albeit earlier assessments missed their complexity.

As stated in Chapter 2, after investigating Sweden's Third World policies, Kenneth Hermele and Karl-Anders Larsson entitled their work *Solidaritet eller Imperialism* (1977) to call attention to the double face of Sweden's policies toward the developing states. They suggested that, on the one hand, Swedish policies toward Third World countries did not differ much from those of other Western/Capitalist states if its economic interests were threatened. On the other hand, Sweden's aid policies were quite 'progressive' compared to the other Western/Capitalist states. Politically radical regimes such as Cuba, national liberation groups such as the African National Congress (ANC), and North Vietnam at the height of its war with the United States received and continue to receive development aid from Sweden.

Hermele and Larsson's contention is, to a large extent, appropriate in the case of Sweden's anti-Apartheid policy. On the one hand, Sweden's trade with South Africa continued to grow in spite of its (Sweden) opposition toward the Apartheid system. On the other hand, Sweden's development aid to the front-line states and the South African liberations forces was quite substantial. As a matter of fact, it was greater than the aid given to the other African regional, geo-political groupings put together (Bangura, 1987, p. 85).

Nevertheless, this book makes a slight departure from Hermele and Larsson's contention: that is, Sweden's policy toward South Africa (in spite of Sweden's economic interests in South Africa) differed from those of many Western/Capitalist states. Sweden was willing to risk its economic interests in South Africa by introducing a number of legislation at the UNGA for concerted international sanctions against South Africa, by its anti-Apartheid voting record which was more impressive than those of many Western/Capitalist states, by its establishment of diplomatic and aid programs in the newly independent front-line states, by its humanitarian aid to the South

African liberation forces, and by its harsh criticism of the South African regime inside and outside of Sweden. Moreover, Sweden's policy toward South Africa did not depend upon its (Sweden) relations with either the other Western/Capitalist states or the Socialist/Communist states.

The reason for Sweden's double-faced policies, however, might have hinged upon what the Swedish Secretariat for Futures Study (SSFS) observed: that is, while many important principles were laid down by the Swedish government and Riksdag (Parliament) concerning the country's relations with the developing countries, Sweden lacked a deliberate and consistently thought-out policy toward those states. Thus, the SSFS concluded, a concerted Swedish policy that would have given prime consideration to the demands of the developing countries was quite impossible. Swedes always found themselves having to strike a balance between their own, sometimes short-term interests and the demands of the developing states. The major issue, therefore, was the degree of consideration Sweden should have given to the demands of the developing countries and to Sweden's own declared support that sometimes took far reaching measures in its aspirations to create a new and fairer global community (SSFS, 1979, p. 46-49).

Indeed, Sweden's policy posture toward Apartheid South Africa hinged upon a number of important factors. To begin with, the total trade between Sweden and South Africa during the Apartheid era was quite insignificant when compared to Sweden's trade with either the United States, the USSR, France, Italy or Canada. There are many factors for this outcome. First, the United States, Canada and the European states were the largest buyers of Sweden's finished steel products. Second, these same countries were the major importers of Swedish automobiles. Third, the United States, the USSR, Canada and the European states were the major consumers of Swedish chemical products. Fourth, the European states were the leading customers, accounting for approximately 60 percent of the total Swedish metalworking industry's engineering products. Fifth, the USSR and the European states were the largest buyers of Sweden's minicomputers and other types of computers. Sixth, the European states were large consumers of Sweden's iron ores. Sweden's supply to the European states was surpassed only by those of the USSR and Canada. Seventh, Sweden in turn imported a large quantity of refined oil products from the European states. Eighth, Sweden bought great amounts of food, tobacco, fats, mineral fuels, chemicals, clothing and footwear from the United States, the USSR, Canada and the European nations (Swedish Institute, 1981 and 1982).

On the other side of the equation, South Africa sold different metal alloys, new materials and fuels along with fruits to Sweden. Sweden in turn sold engineering products and semi-manufactured articles in the form of paper pulp, paper and wood products to South Africa. But what is important about the Swedish goods is that they were required for the industrial expansion of South Africa (LO/TCO, 1975, p. 107).

However, Sweden's trade with South Africa becomes even more insignificant when one looks at, say, the United States' trade with Apartheid South Africa. As Ali Mazrui pointed out,

> Trade between the USA and South Africa has been commensurate in volume. As the two countries entered the 1970s United States exports to South Africa and Namibia were already worth $563 million (17 percent of South Africa's total imports); while the United States imports from the South African Republic totaled $208 million (over 13 per cent of South Africa's total exports, excluding gold) (Mazrui, 1977, p. 165).

The insignificance of Sweden's trade with South Africa is further apparent when one looks at the dramatic increase in the levels of trade between South Africa and its major Western/Capitalist trade partners during the 1980s, for example. South Africa's trade with the United States averaged $3.69 billion during this period; with Britain, it reached $3.62 billion; with West Germany, it reached $3.28 billion; with France, it reached $1.2 billion; and with Japan, it reached $3.24 billion (UN, 1984). These findings, therefore, affirm the contention that South Africa was of secondary importance in Swedish foreign trade.

The Social Democrats maintained an average of 172 seats in a parliamentary system with 349 seats and five competing political parties (Bangura, 1987, p. 85). This means that even at times when the Social Democrats fail to form a government, they can still play a major role in Swedish politics. This result also exemplifies the fact that the Social Democrats have ruled Sweden for 44 years until late 1976, when a non-socialist coalition government was formed by the Center, Liberal and Moderate parties. But the non-socialist coalition government lasted for only two years, and a Liberal minority government served from 1978 until 1979 election–this selection made it possible for the formation of another non-socialist cabinet. However, in May 1981, the moderate party withdrew from the coalition, leaving the Center and Liberal parties in power (Swedish Institute, 1985, p. 2).

Sweden's average anti-Apartheid vote (67 per cent) was relatively higher for the 1960-1984 period when compared to the votes of France (19 per cent), Canada (46 per cent) and Italy (45 per cent). The Swedish vote was superior to that of the United States (23 per cent), reinforcing the claim that America was an ardent supporter of the Pretoria regime. However, the Swedish vote was less impressive when compared to the almost 100 per cent average anti-Apartheid voting record of the USSR (Bangura, 1987, p. 85).

This voting pattern by the Western/Capitalist states seems to buttress Bruce Russett's assertion that over a moderately long period of time, for example, 13 years in certain cases, certain states tend to exhibit strong voting patterns at the UN. As he stated,

About four-fifths of the variation in one year's voting pattern can be predicted by knowing, for the same states, what that pattern looked like in one of the other years. It is not notably lower for the entire 11-year span than for either the shorter period (Russett, 1976, p. 88).

The average Swedish development assistance to the front-line states and the South African liberation groups ($74 million per year) was far greater than the development aid amounts given to the other African regional groupings—Coastal West Africa ($7 million per year), Central and Equatorial West Africa ($0.8 million per year), South Sahara Africa ($2 million per year), East African Island and other East African states ($23 million per year), North Africa ($5 million per year) (Bangura, 1987, p. 86). This finding is a corollary to Roger Leys' suggestion that

Sweden has the most extensive economic interests and aid policy in the heart of the region (Southern Africa), the RSA (Republic of South Africa), and simultaneously pursues the most radical and progressive aid profile both in relationship to the BLS (Botswana, Lesotho and Swaziland) states and in its political material support to the struggle against apartheid (emphasis are mine) (Leys, 1978, p. 56).

Sweden did not establish diplomatic missions in a number of the front-line states for a long time, because one-third of them were under colonial rule up till the mid-1970s and the early 1980s. Angola achieved its independence on November 11, 1975; Mozambique on June 25, 1980; and Zimbabwe on April 18, 1980. Hence, it was not until 1979 that Sweden established a diplomatic mission in Mozambique, and not until 1980 it established those in Angola and Zimbabwe (Bangura, 1987, p. 90).

Thus, no matter its few shortcomings, Sweden's support for the anti-Apartheid movement was quite genuine. And for the millions of South Africans who were being deprived of their basic human needs and rights, forces engaged in the struggle for equality, freedom and independence, must have sincerely cherished Sweden's support. Such support was crucial especially at the time when a concerted international policy to change the status quo in South Africa was lacking.

It was, therefore, not surprising that when late ANC President Oliver Tambo suffered a stroke in 1990 and needed medical treatment, he went to Sweden. It was also only fitting that when former President Nelson Mandela walked out of prison on February 11, 1990, after being incarcerated as a political prisoner in South Africa for 27 years, Sweden was among the first set of countries that he visited. Acknowledging that Sweden was one of the ANC's long-standing allies, Mandela stayed at the beautiful small royal castle of Haga outside of Stockholm where he met visitors from all over Europe. And when Mandela wanted his ex-wife, Winnie, to have the best possible defense against charges of kidnap and assault of Stompie Seipei and five others in December 1988, the Swedes eventually paid much of the heavy cost of the trial in 1991, while part of it was paid by President Muammar Qadaffi of Libya (Sampson, 1999, pp. 407-407, 444).

Thus, those South Africans who struggled against Apartheid still remain grateful to Sweden for its assistance in dismantling the brutal system. For instance, at the beginning of the World Summit on Sustainable Development Heads of Government meeting, the SACC General Secretary presented the Swedish Prime Minister's Senior Policy Advisor, Mr. Roger Hällhag, with a memorandum concerning South Africa's option to purchase 19 JAS 39 Gripen fighter jets. A Swedish translation of the letter, based on the SACC memorandum, was published in the Swedish newspaper, *Göteborgsposten,* on September 3, 2002.

> You have a special place in our hearts. Throughout the terrible years of apartheid oppression, Sweden's people stood in solidarity with South African churches, labour and other civil society organisations, giving moral and material support to those who were struggling for liberation. You joined us in celebrating South Africa's transition to democracy and have invested generously in the reconstruction and development of a new South Africa.

> With the demise of apartheid, we have had to face new challenges to our security and well-being. The economic violence of apartheid policies left a vast gulf between rich and poor, making South Africa one of the most inequitable nations on earth. A majority of our population lives in poverty. The HIV/AIDS pandemic is killing our people at an alarming rate. Today, these crises constitute the greatest threats to the survival of our young and still fragile democracy.

> In 1999, the South African government signed contracts with European armament manufacturers to purchase a range of sophisticated new weapons, including 28

Saab JAS 39 Gripen fighter jets. The national governments of the tendering firms played a pivotal role in securing the contracts. They promoted the weapons, arranged trade and investment offsets to act as incentives, and extended the loans and export credit guarantees necessary to enable South Africa to finance the deal.

In the three years since the deal was completed, a dramatic depreciation in the value of South Africa's currency together with cost escalation clauses in the contracts have combined to nearly double the cost of the package. According to the South African government team that originally assessed the impact of the purchases, only about 30 per cent of the deal can be financed from the national defence budget. The rest must come from other departments. There is thus a real danger that the acquisition of these weapons will further strain our capacity to combat poverty and HIV/AIDS.

Fortunately, portions of the weapons package were optional. In particular, the contract for the Saab JAS 39 Gripen fighters allows the South African government to cancel its order for 19 of the 28 jets until 2004, supposedly without penalty. However, the price of the nine Gripens in the initial batch has been inflated considerably. As a result, the South African government would be faced with the dilemma of justifying the very high unit cost of the fighters if it decides to decline the discounted weapons in the second tranche. Furthermore, given South Africa's desperate need for jobs and investment, the government may be reluctant to lose the countertrade and investment incentives attached to the arms purchases.

We therefore appeal to the government of Sweden to ensure that the people of South Africa will not be penalised if the South African government declines its option to purchase additional Saab fighters. We urge the Swedish government to work with the vendors to find a way to refund the premium paid by South Africa on the first nine fighters if it decides not to make further purchases. We would also ask Sweden's government and industry to demonstrate their continued commitment to South Africa's development by honouring the civilian trade and investment agreements associated with the arms deal, regardless of what decision is made concerning the optional purchases.

We are eternally indebted to the Swedish people for their solidarity with us during the darkest hour of our history. We shall remain always your most valued friends and partners in the global struggle for a just, peaceful and more humane world.

Signed:
Rev. Dr. Molefe TSELE
General Secretary
South African Council of Churches

Cde. Zwelinzima VAVI
General Secretary
Congress of South African Trade Unions

Cde. Abie DITLHAKE
Executive Director
South African NGO Coalition (http://www.sacc.org.za/news/Sweden.html).

Fittingly, Nelson Mandela has been one of the most grateful of South Africans for Sweden's role in helping to end Apartheid. In his Farewell Address to the Swedish Parliament on March 18, 1999, Mandela said the following:

When I spoke to the Swedish parliament nine years ago, almost to the day, it was as a freedom fighter, only weeks out of jail and still denied citizenship in the land of his birth. It was also the first time ever that I had the opportunity to speak in a parliament as the highest institution of democracy. . . .

We know that we stand before those who used their democratic power so that others could have democracy, too. It was here that laws were made and budgets adopted to give effect to the determination of the Swedish people as a whole to be in the forefront of the world-wide campaign to isolate the apartheid regime and to support our struggle for democracy.

It is fitting that what is probably our last official visit to Europe before retirement should include Sweden, which made a contribution to our liberation that was out of all proportion to your size.

Today, South Africa has powerful friends. There is a danger that we may forget those small countries who, when were shunned by almost the entire world, stood with us and in time mobilised the international community. It was therefore important that we should pay this visit before the end of our first democratic government.

We have come to once more thank Sweden from the bottom of our hearts for what you did–the labour movement, NGOs, churches and others, and the million of ordinary Swedish men and women who insisted that the rights they enjoyed should be enjoyed by all people everywhere. Their passionate commitment was reflected in he resolute and remarkable support we had from the Swedish government. . . .

Though the challenges of reconstruction are even greater than those of liberation, and though we have some difficult problems, we face them with confidence, knowing what progress South Africans have made by working together, and knowing tat we have the support of countries like Sweden. . . .

On my return to my country, I will be able to tell my people that in Sweden, as in the other Nordic countries and the Netherlands, we have true friends, indeed, who are ready to work with us in partnership for a better world.

I thank you (http://www.nnn.se/n-model/foreign/mandela.htm).

The essential role the Swedish labor movement in particular played in the struggle against apartheid is still remembered and cherished by South African labor leaders. This is reminiscent of the following speech delivered by CDE James Motlatsi at the South African/Swedish Trade Union Cooperation Seminar on November 25, 1999 at the Gallagher Estate in South Africa.

Meeting together like this with our Comrades from Sweden is a continuation of an essential part of our historical struggle against apartheid. It brings back memories not happy ones, because there was nothing happy about those days-but-important ones, which we should not forget.

Sweden was the strongest ally of the Liberation movement. It is well that we should remember that fact as governments which supported the apartheid regime, are getting in on our act, taking over our companies and monopolizing our trade. We owe nothing to the governments of the major Industrial Countries. They rescued the apartheid government by providing investment after Sharpeville. They shared in the profits from the exploitation of our labour. Their companies refused to recognise black Unions and called in the police to crush our strikes. They obstructed the ANC wherever they could. Remember how Mrs. Thatcher, then Prime Minister of Britain, described the ANC as a terrorist organisation which would never govern South Africa.

It is well that we should remember these facts because Sweden was not like that. It fought against apartheid as if it were one of us. It imposed sanctions against South Africa, persuaded it's companies to disinvest and provided help for the ANC in exile. But what was important from our point of view was that it provided financial and material assistance to struggling Unions in this Country at a time when repression was at its most intense. Both the NUM and NUMSA owe a great debt to Sweden for without its help, we may not have succeeded in surviving. Sweden gave NUM finance to launch a shaft stewards' training scheme which produced cadres for the struggle.

Funds we received were earmarked for specific projects but there were no strings attached. Sweden wanted nothing in return. We designed the projects and accounted for the expenditures. Handling the funds was a lesson in accountancy and administration, which we were denied by apartheid in other spheres of life. This support continued for us until we were able to be self-sufficient.

There is a lesson here for South Africa, and for other Third World Countries. Western industrial donor Countries, the IMF and the World Bank which provided aid and investment funds for Third World Countries, never give them without imposing conditions about how they should apply them and organise their societies. The conditions, without exception, have been counterproductive for they have ignored their culture, the state of their economies and their specific economic and political conditions. They have wanted to impose the images of their own societies on us so that they can control us more effectively for their own interests. There is nothing benevolent or good intentioned about the big powers. They want to dominate, exploit and suck us dry and in doing it they corrupt us. Corruption is an import from the West

 Now if they treated us like the Sweden treated us, then, it would be a wholly different situation. We would formulate our own policies and use the funds with strict accountability. We would undertake projects with timetables. Everything would be done in a disciplinary way. There would be no corruption. Our societies would develop as we wished them to develop, using state mechanisms, public ownership and the market mechanism in the combinations best suited to our conditions and shaped by our own aspirations.

But what of our future relationships with the Swedish Metal Workers Union? Quite clearly in whatever we do, we shall be the main beneficiaries but we would like our activities to benefit both sides wherever possible. Our problems in South Africa are momentous but, given the opportunity, we can tackle them as mature, responsible organisations in the open with the co-operation of the government. The situation could hardly be more different from those days in the 1980s.

I would like us to join with the Swedish Unions to set new programs for our mutual benefit. As a means of executing these programs, I suggest that we establish joint workshops to meet alternately in South Africa and Sweden. They could, I believe, usefully discuss the trading relationships between our two countries with the intention of identifying ways and means of intensifying and expanding them. From our side, we could promote the return of Swedish Companies to South Africa and suggest practical ways of expanding their sales. We desperately need to expand our export markets and would like to hear how Sweden could assist us.

There are problems which are specific to South Africa where Sweden could possibly assist. One of the legacies of apartheid, which is preventing our economic development, is the lack of skills in our work forces. We need training programs in a range of occupations which will provide us with sufficiently skilled workers to expand our traditional industries and venture into new high technological ones. We have little experience in skills training whereas Sweden has an abundance of it.

Apartheid left many legacies. If I had to relate them all I would be here for weeks or months. In order to save time, I will just mention one more. It is that we have been left with a wholly inadequate tertiary education system so that we have no means of complementing skill training programs and of taking the skills of our young people a stage further towards the levels of occupational competency that are present in the developed industrial countries. We are in a hurry. We do not have the time or the resources to emulate those countries by building educational institutions which would do the trick. We have to find other ways. We look to Sweden with its wealth of educational experience to assist us.

I would like to end by saying that it gives me and my Union enormous pleasure to be able to receive you, our Swedish friends, in an open democratic South African Society so that you can see the measure of your contributions to the changes that have taken place in such a short space of time.

I THANK YOU(http://www.num.org.za/News/misc/swedish.htm).

Swedish political leaders are still committed to seeing democracy and a better quality of life thrive in South Africa and other countries. In her speech at the World Conference against Racism, Racial Discrimination, Xenophobia and Related Intolerance held in Durban, South Africa from August 31 to September 7, 2001, Her Excellency Mona Sahlin, Minister of Industry, Employment and Communications, made the following statement:

President,
Your Excellencies,
Heads of State and Government,
Honourable Ministers, Excellencies, Ambassadors,
Distinguished guests,
Ladies and Gentlemen,

My Government is very grateful to the Government of South Africa for hosting this important Conference. It is appropriate and perhaps no coincidence that we are meeting here today to discuss racism. The tragedy of discrimination on the basis of colour has nowhere been more clearly shown than in apartheid South Africa. And indeed, apartheid was a system that could not be reformed. It had to be abolished. In his last foreign policy speech, the former Swedish Prime Minister Olof Palme stated this, and added "If the rest of the world decides, if people all over the world decide that apartheid is to be abolished, the system will disappear."

Sweden worked for the isolation of the apartheid regime. We supported the struggle against apartheid. We supported the unique Truth and Reconciliation effort made in South Africa, we are partners with the new democratic government of South Africa in reform and development. We think it is appropriate that we learn from the South African experience as we continue to guard against all forms of racism, racial discrimination, xenophobia and related intolerance.

These are serious threats to the future of all humanity. Unfortunately, no country in the world is free of these scourges. Governments have the primary responsibility for fighting racism, racial discrimination, xenophobia and related intolerance. But the shared responsibility of the international community must also be emphasised. If we cannot create a world in which everyone is respected and treated equally, we will endanger the future of every individual.

This conference is perhaps the greatest manifestation ever of the international community's determination to act against these four evils. What we say and decide here in Durban will inspire people all over the world to make greater efforts to achieve more just societies. The world conference will be a strong mobilising factor to this end.

But what we do not say and decide here in Durban is equally important. We must not allow differences of opinion to hinder us in our task of giving concrete direction for continued efforts throughout the world to counteract different forms of intolerance. We must not fail to grasp this historic opportunity.

The point of departure must be our joint ambition to create societies where all individuals have the same rights and are treated equally regardless of race, colour, descent, national or ethnic origin, religion, language, gender, sexual orientation or any other status.

I would also like to take this opportunity to express our regrets that this conference has been overshadowed by current conflict situations. As the High Commissioner for Human Rights expressed in her statement of yesterday, I believe that this conference is not the right forum to sort out the different problems on the international agenda.

This Conference is about combating contemporary forms of racism, racial discrimination, xenophobia and related intolerance. In doing this we must also deal with history and, however difficult and painful, confront our past. This is important to all of us, not only for reconciliation but also for healing and for building bridges to the future. The grave consequences of past injustices emanating from slavery, slave trade and colonialism are still felt and there are many unhealed wounds.

Regrettably, racism, racial discrimination, xenophobia and related intolerance in Sweden, as in many other countries, have found more and more aggressive expression. In recent years we have witnessed an increase in violence and harassment against immigrants, homosexuals, Jews and Roma. We have seen journalists, policemen and politicians attacked. We are extremely concerned about this development, which is an attack not only on these individuals but also on our democratic society and our fundamental belief in the concept of the equal worth of all people.

Governments have the primary responsibility for working to oppose and combat racism, racial discrimination, xenophobia and related intolerance. The Swedish Government regards this task as one of its most important duties. Efforts to strengthen commitment have been vigorously pursued for many years.

In this context I would like to stress that it is utterly important that all anti-racist policies must be gender-sensitive, since racism, racial discrimination, xenophobia and related intolerance affect women and men in different ways.

One way of achieving this commitment is through the adoption of national action plans ensuring that concerted efforts become more effective, more long-term and more structured. In February 2001, the Swedish Government adopted such a national action plan against racism, xenophobia, homophobia and discrimination. The purpose of the plan is to mobilise the whole of society at all levels - government agencies, local and county council authorities, trade union and employer organisations, companies and business associations, NGOs and the general public - in order to fight for a Swede n where each individual is respected, regardless of colour, ethnic or national origin, religious belief or sexual orientation.

Education and a raising of awareness are essential tools in the fight against racism, racial discrimination, xenophobia and related intolerance. In this regard, I would like to mention the Living History project, initiated by the Swedish Prime Minister. The project aims at increasing awareness of history and of how the past, the present and the future are intimately related. It aims at making sure that younger generations do not forget about the past. A book informing about the horrors of the Holocaust has been offered to every schoolchild. Building on this project, the Swedish Government plans to set up a "centre of excellence" in order to support the promotion of democracy, tolerance and human rights. As examples of the Swedish Government's contribution to international cooperation in this area, let me also mention the Stockholm International Forum on the Holocaust, held in January 2000, and the Stockholm International Forum on Combating Intolerance, held in January, 2001.

Our common efforts, based on international solidarity and partnership, are important tools for combating poverty and promoting a sustainable development. They will ensure that all countries are integrated into the world economy. This will contribute towards preventing the vicious circle of racism, racial discrimination, xenophobia and related intolerance.

Mr/Madam Chair
Individuals may suffer from discrimination on the grounds of race, colour, descent or national or ethnic origin. Finally, let me draw your attention to individuals whose situation is aggravated by the fact that they suffer discrimination on other grounds also, such as their sexual orientation.

Sexual orientation represents an important part of a person's identity, as does gender or ethnic background. The Universal Declaration on Human Rights states that all human beings are born equal in dignity and rights. For the Swedish Government it is self-evident that all human beings must be treated equally, irrespective of their sexual orientation.

Sexual relations between people of the same gender are criminal offences in more than 70 countries and in some of these, the death penalty is imposed. Violence by the police and other representatives of the state is common. Violations by "ordinary people" at school, in the workplace or on the street are also often reported.

Mr/Madam Chair
I would like to quote from a recent Amnesty International report: "In the case of gays, history and experience teach us that the scarring comes not from poverty or powerlessness, but from invisibility. It is the tainting of desire, it is the attribution of perversity and shame to spontaneous bodily affection, it is the prohibition of the expression of love, it is the denial of full moral citizenship in society because you are what you are, that impinges on the dignity and self-worth of a group."

Hatred and contempt against people because of their sexual orientation is common among extreme right wing and racist groups. Constantly homosexuals and people with foreign background are both target groups for hate crime among many racists. Protection and the rights of these people must be strengthened.

I am convinced that some time in the future, people will be respected for what they are, regardless of their sexual orientation.

Mr/Madam Chairman
On behalf of the Swedish Government, I would like to extend our sincere appreciation and congratulations to the Government of South Africa for its role in preparing and hosting this conference.

We are confident that it will prove to be a landmark in global efforts to promote a better world for all people. But we must also remember that the conference, and what we decide here, is only the beginning of our work. The long-term success of this conference will depend on ourselves. It is up to all of us, when we return home, to do all that we can to realise the promises made in Durban. We owe this to ourselves, to our children and to the generations to come.

Thank you very much (http://un.org/WCAR/statements/swedenE.htm).

Does the account of Swedish policy toward Apartheid South Africa I have provided in this book give us reason to proffer a 'Swedish model' which differs from those of other countries? If so what is distinctive about this model? Indeed, there is no simple answer to this question. Nonetheless, the perspective offered by Stig Hadenius on a similar question almost 20 years ago is till instructive.

For over half a century, Swedish politics has been characterized by great stability. The roles of the various political parties have not changed much. The parties that dominated the Riksdag 60 years ago still do. Changes in people's voting have not varied much (Hadenius, 1985, p. 165).

Many important political decisions have been made through compromise. Over the decades, there has been a common desire by all political parties to reach so-called broad solutions in many areas, especially foreign policy, defense and constitutional reform. Political parties have made national interest a priority over their own self-interests (Hadenius, 1985, p. 165).

The Swedish model was tarnished in the 1970s, as relations between labor and management became strained. A series of regulations on the labor market was responsible for the strain. Nonetheless, the non-socialist governments in power between 1976 and 1982 did not attempt to change the Swedish welfare state. Instead, they vowed to defend it in an attempt to repair its shortcomings–growing bureaucracy, high taxes and increasing restrictions on personal freedom (Hadenius, 1985, p. 166-167).

The Swedish welfare state provides free education through graduate school level, virtually free medical care, unemployment compensation, sick pay, various forms of support to families with children, housing allowances, etc. Even tough the public sector has grown more rapidly in Sweden than in any other country, most Swedes consider the development a positive one for several reasons: (a) the differences between the sexes on the labor market have narrowed, (b) class differences have become smaller, (c) it is easier for children from working class homes to obtain a higher education, and (d) political participation has increased (Hadenius, 1985, p. 167).

Critics of the Social Democrats point to the adverse effects of a lack of competition in many sectors of the economy, the growth of the bureaucracy and the excessively high costs for public services. Some even blame many of the negative aspects of the modern industrial state–e.g., drug abuse, suicide, etc.–on the welfare state. The critics also argue that high taxes result in a flourishing underground economy and that the comprehensive welfare safety net discourages individuals from taking sufficient responsibility for their own lives (Hadenius, 1985, p. 169).

The Social Democrats respond by saying that government intervention does not necessarily reduce individual freedom. They extended social welfare system offers economic security. The expansion of the educational system allows young people greater freedom of choice. The supplementary pension reform means that employees can change jobs without fear of losing their income-related pension benefits, as often happens in other countries. All this, the Social Democrats argue, guarantees greater freedom of choice (Hadenius, 1985, p. 169).

Hence, the image of the Swedish model is a fragmented one. The question, then, is the following: How will it will hold up in the future? Sweden has one advantage over many other Western countries: Its strong special interest organizations and stable political party structure have been positive factors in both the labor market and in politics (Hadenius, 1985, p. 169).

During the early 1980s, Swedish industry showed its competitive strength. A concerted effort involving both corporate management and representatives of national and local governments has often been employed in dealing with structural changes. Its heavy dependence on foreign trade means that Sweden must hold its own in world markets in order to maintain its prosperity. Being highly sensitive to fluctuations in global economic conditions, Sweden must compete primarily by offering quality high-tech goods and services (Hadenius, 1985, p. 170).

For more than 70 years, the Swedish model that evolved also included a non-aligned foreign policy. However, this did not mean that Sweden assumed a passive attitude toward events beyond its borders. The country was active both as a mediator in various conflicts–from Folke Bernadotte's mission in Palestine to Olof Palme's UN mission in the Iran-Iraq war. It took initiatives for promoting peace, including the Undén Plan for a non-nuclear weapons club and the promotion of the proposal for a corridor in Europe free of battle field nuclear weapons. It also took a stand in favor of the right of self-determination of relatively small nations that were drawn into conflicts involving superpowers–for example, Vietnam, Afghanistan and the countries of Central America (Hadenius, 1985, p. 170).

Consensus among the political parties in foreign policy and security matters was the rule. For instance, those who advocated Swedish membership into the North Atlantic Treaty Organization (NATO) were not supported by any party in the Riksdag. Instead, all the parties represented in the parliament pledged their support for the policy of non-alignment (Hadenius, 1985, p. 170).

With the emergence of the United States as the sole superpower in the 21st Century, the erosion of administrative practices and centralized bargaining, the abandonment of neutrality and the reduction of the welfare state, it is evident that Swedes are starting to scribble a new chapter in their uniquely peaceful economic, political and social history. It is more likely that Sweden will move economically and politically towards the rest of Europe, leaving behind its egalitarian hallmark. This move will be undergirded by a spirit of compromise among the economic and political elite. Those Swedes who are vulnerable to the shortcomings of globalization will resist the move.

No matter the push-pull factors, Sweden's long historical tradition will continue to edge it towards the preservation of its national independence and peace. Sweden has never in modern times been ruled by a foreign power or occupied by foreign troops. Sweden did not participate in the two World Wars, and none of the majors powers engaged in those wars attacked Sweden. Therefore, the basing of Sweden's foreign and defense policies on neutrality was successful.

Sweden must continue to take a great interest in all attempts to create an international legal system to safeguard the integrity and independence of small nations. The fact that there are many examples of states infringing the basic rules of international coexistence is no reason for Sweden not to assert the continued validity of these rules. At the same time, it should avoid all acts that would constitute a threat to the security of other countries. Sweden has always been aware of the importance of fostering the will and the ability to assert its independence and integrity in all situations, and it must continue to do so.

Sweden must continue the principal function of its total defense to preserve peace by having such a structure, state of readiness and the strength that an aggressor's losses and other sacrifices in connection with an attempt to exploit Swedish territory would not be in a reasonable proportion to the gains. A total defense of this nature will hinge upon a substantial contribution to peace and stability and the limiting of major power presence in Europe in peacetime and during international crises. Such a strategy is also imperative, if Sweden's peaceful approach is to be respected in the event of war on the continent.

Sweden must continue to act in accordance with its own judgment in deciding the content of its foreign policy in each situation. Such a course will be understood and respected by other states. The social and cultural dimensions of Sweden's security policy must remain paramount. If the living conditions of large sectors of the population deteriorate, if there are growing social differences and anxiety for the future, the citizens' sense of solidarity with the society that leaders wish to defend will be undermined. Efforts to promote social welfare in Sweden must be continued in order to safeguard the nation's peace and independence. Open cultural contacts with other countries must also be continued, as cultural awareness strengthens citizens' confidence and their will to defend their nation.

Reducing the risk of being drawn into war and other conflicts must remain vital to Sweden. The use of nuclear weapons against Sweden would put its very survival at stake. To reduce this likelihood, Sweden must continue to push for the reduction, if not elimination, of such weapons of mass destruction.

In essence, Sweden's foreign and security policies must contribute to disarmament and reconciliation within and between countries. Sweden must also continue to pursue foreign and defense policies designed to enable the nation to withstand pressure and demands, to counter violations of Swedish territory, and to defend itself if attacked.

Postscript

The Murder of Anna Lindh

As I was doing the final revisions for this book, the news came that 46-year-old Swedish Foreign Minister Anna Lindh had died at Karolinska Hospital in Stockholm, Sweden. Lindh was stabbed in the chest, stomach and arms on September 10, 2003, while she was shopping at the Nordiska Kompaniet store in Stockholm. She spent the night in surgery for more than 10 hours, as doctors tried unsuccessfully to save her life, and died the following day (September 11, 2003). As of this writing, her attacker and the motive for the killing remain unknown. Like most Swedish politicians, Lindh did not have a bodyguard. Her killing has stirred memories of the assassination of her role model and mentor, Olof Palme, in 1986 discussed in Chapter 6 of this book (http://news.bbc.co.uk).

The hunt for Lindh's killer has not been successful, with Swedish police announcing on September 12, 2003 that they had released a 32-year-old man once perceived as the prime suspect, after questioning him in connection with the murder. Stockholm police spokesperson Bjoern Pihlblad was quoted as saying that "We have a number of people that we are investigating, we have not singled out a suspect" (http://www.567.co.za).

Ylva Anna Maria Lindh was born on June 19, 1957 in Enskede, a south-eastern suburb of Stockholm. She was the daughter of Staffan Lindh, an artist, and Nancy Lindh, a teacher. Anna Lindh received her law degree from the University of Uppsala in 1982 and worked for six months at the district court before winning a seat in parliament running as a Social Democrat that same year. In 1991, she married another Social Democrat politician, Bo Holmberg, a former government minister who is now the county governor in Sodermanland, south of Stockholm. He and their two sons, Filip and David, survive her (wysiwyg://77http://www.telegraph, wysiwyg://61/http://www. guardian.co).

Lindh got involved in politics at the very young age of 12 at Sanobro School in Enkoping, a town to the west of Stockholm, when she was elected president of the local Social Democratic youth club. By the time she was 20, she had become a local councillor. Between 1984 and 1990, she was president of the Swedish Social Democratic party's youth movement, having also served as vice chairperson of the International Union of Socialist Youth (1987-89). She was a member of her party's influential executive committee from 1991, a city councillor for culture in Stockholm from 1991 to 1994, and then minister for the environment until 1998, when she was appointed foreign minister. Lindh became one of Sweden's most popular politicians, widely tipped as the person to succeed Prime Minister Goran Persson as leader of the Social Democratic Party, and possibly becoming her country's next Prime Minister. She possessed all of the features that Swedes tend to admire in their leaders: brilliant, but unassuming, and full of opinions about how other countries should behave (wysiwyg://77http://www/telegraph, wysiwyg: //61/http://www.guardian.co).

As a senior member of of the ruling Social Democratic Party, Lindh emerged as one of the government's leading figures in its faltering campaign to persuade the country's nine million citizens to adopt the euro as the nation's currency. Nicknamed the 'Queen of the Yes Campaign,' she was seen as the single currency's most persuasive advocate. Her smiling photograph was pasted on bus stops and telephone booths in every city and town in Sweden. While Persson failed to catch the public's imagination, Lindh seized the initiative with warnings that foreign investment would dry up and tens of thousands of jobs would be lost if Swedes delivered a 'No' vote. In recent months, she persuaded Greek Foreign Minister George Papandreou and German Foreign Minister Joschka Fischer to go to Sweden to add their voices to the pro-euro campaign, in order to strengthen her government's argument that staying out of the euro would mean diplomatic isolation for Sweden (wysiwyg://77http://www.telegraph, wysiwyg://61/http://www.guardian.co). The euro referendum was defeated on September 14, 2003.

Lindh was said to have been a 'woman without enemies,' and her keen mind and cheerful demeanor won her many friends at home and abroad. In tune with Sweden's consensus-minded and egalitarian culture, Lindh could be seen traveling everywhere by public transportation and could even be seen sitting on the carriage floor thumbing through policy documents if there were no empty seats on the crowded train back to her constituency in Nykoping. Many diplomats were wary when the young and radical Lindh first stepped into their gilded ministry. But resistance melted quickly away, and she enjoyed strong support from her staff. It was frustratingly hard for journalists to dig out scandals from her ministry, because there were none and she enjoyed tremendous loyalty. Lindh's ability to laugh at herself contributed to her persona. The Swedish daily *Svenska Dagbladet* once ran a photograph of her looking cross-eyed while checking her glasses. Many readers took offence on her behalf, but she wrote the editors of the newspaper stating that it was funny. American Secretary of State Colin Powell once said that there were three things he particularly liked about Sweden: 'Abba, Volvo and Anna.' To which she responded: 'Why do I only come in third?' (wysiwyg://77http://www. telegraph, wysiwyg://61/http://www.guardian.co).

Lindh often stuck out from the dull crowd of men in dark suits at international summits. A blonde, sometimes carrying her papers in a rucksack, was a rare sight in those settings. But it was more than her looks. She managed to combine the casual style with a sharp intellect, and knew when to employ the one or the other. Her skills were put to the test during the Swedish presidency of the European Union in the spring of 2001, when war was looming in Macedonia. She was instrumental in bringing the European Union's usually disparate foreign policy into the harmonized action that prevented the conflict (wysiwyg://77http://www.telegraph, wysiwyg://61/ http://www. guardian.co).

Lindh's appointment as foreign minister came in the midst of a process of soul-searching within the Social Democratic movement on how to rejuvenate party policy and strengthen Sweden's position in the European Union. Dubbed by the media as 'Persson's Crown Princess,' Lindh quickly established a reputation of championing human rights and for blunt criticisms of violators, including some of Sweden's allies. In Moscow, she criticized Russian actions in Chechnya; in Washington, DC, she castigated Americans for their treatment of Afghan war prisoners in Guantanamo Bay. Her sharp criticism of the United States struck a chord that has vibrated loudly in Sweden since the days of the Vietnam war and Palme. She described George W. Bush as a 'lone ranger' for going to war with Iraq. However, she stopped short of throwing Sweden's weight behind the French-led opposition against the war. While she was opposed to the war on the grounds that it had not been sanctioned by the United Nations, Lindh was not opposed to war in principle. After the attacks in New York and Washington, DC on September 11, 2001, she expressed support for the American-led war on global terrorism; and in January of 2003, she told members of the Parliament that the threat of military action was necessary to pressure Saddam Hussein into complying with United Nations resolutions. In recent months, Lindh admonished Italian Prime Minister Silvio Berlusconi for comparing a German member of parliament to a Nazi concentration camp guard and suggested that Berlusconi's behavior was a good argument for scrapping the European Union's rotating presidency. Later, she stated that Italy under Berlusconi's rule was not fit to run the European Union's presidency at a time when a new constitution is to be negotiated.

While her remarks might not have endeared her to many Italians, most of her colleagues in the council of ministers held similar sentiments but shied away from voicing them publicly (wysiwyg://77http://www.telegraph, wysiwyg://61/http://www. guardian.co).

Lindh was an outspoken critic of Israeli Prime Minister Ariel Sharon's policy towards the Palestinians. She stated her government's position as follows: 'Our stand is firm and clear. Israeli settlement in the West Bank must go; there must be a Palestinian state; Israel must vacate all occupied areas on the West Bank and Gaza Strip and end all extra-territorial executions and attacks on Palestinians' (wysiwyg://77http://www.telegraph). Lindh was also among the first to call for Zimbabwean President Robert Mugabe's resignation after his policy to resettle Blacks on White-owned farms showed a blatant disregard for the rule of law. She also rebuked the Turkish government for its treatment of Kurds and met with several high-profile human rights groups when she visited the country in early 2000 (http://www.worldlink.co.uk).

An important aspect of Lindh's political orientation was her unwavering belief in the democratic process, albeit she had serious reservations about globalization. The following speech she made at the Institute for Democracy and Electoral Assistance in the Riksdag on December 9, 1999 seems to underscore that belief:

Ladies and gentlemen,
I am very pleased to be here, because this is an important seminar, but also because it gives me the opportunity to meet old friends like Thorvald Stoltenberg.

Dear friends,
During the last ten years we have witnessed a remarkable progress for democracy and democratic values. Many countries have abandoned dictatorship and authoritarian rule. They have entered the complex road to democratic government and to a change of attitudes that must involve the entire population.

Today, almost all European countries are democratic, and the military dictators in Latin America have surrendered to elected presidents. In Africa apartheid and one-party systems have lost ground to the benefit of strengthened democracy. And in Asia, the fourth most populous nation of the world, Indonesia, have elected a president this autumn in a democratic process.

When the Soviet-empire collapsed, it was also the end of the cold war. The collapse paved the way for democratization - not only because the Soviet Union and the Eastern European countries could develop into democracies, but also because the US reduced their more or less open support to right-wing authoritarian regimes, when the geopolitical rivalry between the superpowers came to an end.

The conquests of democracy are substantial and important, but have so far not been enough to bring about peace.

I think that one reason might be that we have not adapted to the new situation and realised that we now have better possibilities to use democracy for conflict-prevention. During the cold war nations were pawns in a game of interest-spheres–and it was difficult then to intervene with conflict-preventing measures. Now the international community and the UN can discuss, act and react toward individual countries, both in the field of democracy and in conflict-prevention.

We all know that when a conflict has escalated into open violence, it is hard to revert to dialogue. Therefore, we must act at a much earlier stage, before a conflict deteriorates into armed violence. This is a moral, humanitarian and economic imperative–a global responsibility. We need long-term strategies, but also better instruments to deal with the present.

The Swedish Social Democratic Government presented an action plan in May this year, with the aim to strengthen our common ability of preventive measures–changing the focus from crisis management to early preventive action. The plan defines several goals for such efforts:

-To promote a culture of prevention, with the objective to ensure that early prevention becomes the natural response to early warning signals.

-To identify structural risk factors and the causes of conflict, and to take appropriate action. Human rights violations, for example, are often a sign that armed conflict may be about to break out.

-To develop and strengthen the international system of norms and its implementation, as well as the international institutional framework and its preventive instruments.

Dear friends,
I am convinced that democracy, if taken seriously, is both an excellent instrument for conflict-prevention and a prerequisite for lasting peace.

Is democracy the road to peace? I would say it is–even if it is not an obvious or easy road.

1. It is likely to believe that countries with a practice of tolerance and peaceful conflict-resolution within their societies, will act according to the same values internationally.

2. Although democratic decision-making does not automatically solve the problems of a society, democracies seldom let conflicts escalate into violence. Democracies have the possibilities to develop the institutions, resources and flexibility needed to manage conflicts peacefully.

3. Long-term stability and peace require economic and social development, justice and respect for human rights. Democracies are better equipped to enhance such policies.

But democracy also faces new threats, in the time of globalization.

Increased trade and investment, and the rapid movement of capital has promoted growth and led to a decrease in the share of poor during the 1990-ties. But at the same time, the gaps between rich and poor countries, and between rich and poor within countries, have increased.

Today, the capital of the two-hundred most wealthy individuals exceeds the incomes of about 2,5 billion people.

- Globalization promotes growth and wealth - but also growing gaps.

- Globalization can promote human rights and democracy when information and ideas are easily spread by means of mass-communication.

But too often globalization mean a common market economy—without global values such as respect for human rights in common. Then the globalization means immense power of an anonymous, irresponsible and short-sighted market.

Dear friends,
Never before in history, there have been as many democracies in the world as today, on the threshold to the new millennium. This gives us reason to look at the new century with some confidence. But we need to use the new possibilities democracy provides us with, to strengthen conflict-prevention, and we need to strengthen democracy in order to prevent new gaps in the world economy, and new threats to peace. We need to adapt to the new situation!
Thank you! (http://www.student.sap.se/burma/aktuelt_konf_dok.htm).

Another important aspect of Lindh's political orientation was the belief in working hard to accomplish goals. She worked tirelessly to ensure that Sweden attains the United Nations' goal of allocating 0.7 per cent of GNP to development aid in 1999 and 0.8 per cent in 2000. Only a few other countries came close to meeting these targets (http://www.worldlink.co.uk).

As a protégée of Palme, Lindh was a staunch supporter of his mentor's anti-Apartheid actions and an admirer of Nelson Mandela's peaceful approach to dealing with the South African situation when he became President. Following her country's long-term support of the anti-Apartheid movement, Lindh provided significant assistance to the ruling ANC government. Recently, she signed a $74 million agreement with Mbeki to provide more housing for the poor and better research facilities for the universities (http://www.worldlink.co.uk). Her admiration for Mandela's peaceful approach is evident from the following excerpt in her speech at the Conference on the situation in Burma held in Stockholm on March 18, 1999: 'Even if we are going to discuss the current situation in Burma today–indeed a very depressing one–I feel optimistic, since I have just met with President Nelson Mandela, a person so full of hope and confidence. The struggle for democracy and human dignity in South Africa shows us that oppression can be overcome–and that change is possible' (http://www.student.sap.se).

It was only fitting that on September 11, 2003, a few minutes after receiving the news that Lindh had died, South African President Thabo Mbeki and his foreign minister, Nkosazana Dlamini-Zuma, conveyed their condolences to the Swedish government and people. In the words of Mbeki, 'It is with great shock and outrage that the government and people of South Africa learnt of the death of Ms Anna Lindh...following a brutal attack on her....Ms Lindh personally contributed much to promoting international peace, and was seen as a great friend to South Africa.' Dlamini-Zuma expressed similar sentiments when she stated that 'An unforgivable crime has been visited once more on the people of Sweden.' In paying tribute to Lindh, Dlamini-Zuma said that Lindh had a bright future ahead of her and possessed a 'gift and finesse of diplomacy... Her death cannot but remind the entire democratic world of a similar crime committed against the great son of Sweden, Prime Minister Olof Palme.' Dlamini-Zuma continued by stating her hope that the Swedish government would ensure that Lindh's murderer would face the 'full might of the law.' She concluded by urging that 'The greatest tribute that we can pay Anna is to intensify our efforts to fulfill her vision to create a better and safer world in which we can live in peace and harmony without fear of another human being' (http://www.iol.co.za).

Bibliography

Alexandroff, Alan S. (1981). *The Logic of Diplomacy*. Beverly Hills, California: Sage Publications.

Alker, Hayward R., Jr. and Bruce M. Russett. (1965). *World Politics in the General Assembly*. New Haven, Connecticut: Yale University Press.

Andersson, Invar and Weibul, Jörgen. (1980). *Swedish History in Brief*. Sodertalje, Sweden: Wiking Tryckeri AB.

Andrén, Nils. (1967). *Power-Balance and Non-Alignment*. Stockholm, Sweden: Almqvist and Wiksell.

Andrén, Nils. (1982). *Essays on Swedish Security in the Nordic Environment*. Stockholm, Sweden: The Swedish Defense Research Institute.

Andromidas, Dean. (February 24, 1997). Presentation for EIR Seminar, Stockholm. Available: http://www.nysol.se/arkiv/politik/dean.html

Anglin, D. et. al. (1978). *Canada, Scandinavia and Southern Africa*. Uppsala, Sweden: Uppsala Offsetcenter AB.

Anton, Thomas J. (1980). *Administered Politics*. Boston, Massachusetts: Martinus Nijhoff Publishing.

Back, P. E. (1976). *Aammanslutningarnas roll i politiken, 1870-1910*. Skelleftea, Sweden: Västerbottens Tryckeri.

Bangura, Abdul Karim. (1987). *A Quantitative Analysis of Sweden's Foreign Policy Toward South Africa: A Treatise on Anti-Apartheid* (Doctoral Dissertation, Howard University, Washington, DC).

Beckman, Björn. (1978). *Aid and Foreign Investment: The Swedish Case*. Uppsala, Sweden: Uppsala University Press.

Berglund, S. and U. Lindstrom. (1978). *The Scandinavia Party System(s)*. Lund, Sweden: Studenliteratur.

Bhagwati, Jagdish N. (1970). *Amount and Sharing of Aid* (Monograph #. 2). Washington, DC: Overseas Development Co-operation.

Bhattacharya, Anindya K. (1976). *Foreign Trade and International Development*. Lexington, Massachusetts: Lexington Books.

Blake, David H. and Robert S. Walters. (1976). *The Politics of Global Economic Relations*. Englewood Cliffs, New Jersey: Prentice-Hall, Inc.

Board, Jr., Joseph B. (1970). *The Government and Politics of Sweden*. Boston, Massachusetts: Houghton and Mifflin Co.

Boyce, Peter J. (1977). *Foreign Affairs for New States.* New York, New York: St. Martin's Press.

Brandt, Willy (Commission). (1980). *North-South: A Program for Survival.* Cambridge, Massachusetts: MIT Press.

Brown, Lester R. (1981). *Building a Sustainable Society.* New York, New York: W. W. Norton and Co.

Castles, Francis G. (1977). Scandinavian social democracy: Achievements and origins (unpublished report presented to the ECPR workshop on Social Democratic Parties, Berlin, March 28-April 1).

Cenry, Karl. (1977). *Scandinavia at the Polls.* Washington, DC: AEIPP Research.

Childs, Marquis Q. (1980). *Sweden: The Middle Way on Trial.* New Haven, Connecticut: Yale University Press.

Clarke, D. G. (1981). *Economic Sanctions on South Africa.* London, England: Stanhope Press.

Coplin, W. and C. Kegley, Jr., eds. (1971). *A Multi-Method Introduction to International Politics.* Chicago, Illinois: Markham Publishing Co.

Couloumbis, Theodore A. and James H. Wolfe. (1978). *Introduction to International Relations.* Englewood Cliffs, New Jersey: Prentice-Hall, Inc.

Dahl, Robert. (1957). The concept of power. *Behavioral Sciences* 2:201-205.

Dallenbrandt, J. Å. and V. Pestoff. (1979). Elites as gatekeepers: Democratic and oligargic tendencies in Swedish cooperative society. *Statsventenskapliga Tidskrift, 1980.*

De Jonge, Klass. South African Links in the Murder of Olof Palme. Available: http://www.totse.com/en/politics/the_world_beyond_the_usa/167128.html

Deutsch, Karl. (1968). *The Analysis of International Relations.* Englewood Cliffs, New Jersey: Prentice-Hall, Inc.

Dyer, Gwyne. (1985). Palme, the Sanctimonious Swede. *The Washington Times.* Tuesday, June 4:11A.

Economist, The. (1982). 285, 7259, October 16-22:67.

Ekerberge, M. (1981). Perspectiver på organiseringen av forhaldet mellon staten og organissasjonere i representative Konstitutusjonelle System. *Nordiska Statvetenskapliga Konferens i Åbo,* Oslo, Norway.

Giarini, Oric and Henri Loubergé. (1978). *The Diminishing Returns of Technology.* Oxford, England: Oxford University Press.

Hadenius, Stig (1985). *Swedish Politics During the 20th Century.* Stockholm, Sweden: Swedish Institute.

Hagström, Nidia and Sarah Roxström. (September 30, 1996). The Swedish Press on the South African Connection. Available: http://www.lysator.liu.se/nordic/murder/radiosweden_press.html

Hanna, Mike. (October 21, 1996). Police Implicate Former President in Apartheid-Era Assassination. Available: http://www.cnn.com/WORLD/9610/21/south.africa.truth/

Hayter, Teresa. (1981). *The Creation of World Poverty.* London, England: Pluto Press.

Hayter, Teresa. (1971). *Aid as Imperialism.* Middlesex, England: Penguin Books Ltd.

Hayter, Teresa and Catherine Watson. (1985). *Aid: Rhetoric and Reality*. London, England: Pluto Press.

Heck, Harold J. (1972). *International Trade*. United States: American Management Association Inc.

Heilbroner, Robert L. (1970). *The Making of Economic Society*. Old Tappan, New Jersey: Prentice-Hall International Inc.

Hermele, Kenneth and Karl-Anders Larsson. (1977). *Solidaritet eller Imperialism*. Stockholm, Sweden: Liber.

Hettne, Björn. (1978). *Current Issues in Development Theory*. Stockholm, Sweden: SAREC Report, R5.

Hettne, Björn and Peter Wallensteen. (1978). *Emerging Trends in Development Theory*. Stockholm, Sweden: SAREC Report, R3.

Himmelstrand, Ulf et al. (1982). *Beyond Welfare Capitalism*. Stockholm, Sweden: Liber.

Holst, Johan Jørgen, ed. (1973). *Five Roads to Nordic Security*. Oslo, Norway: Universitetforlaget.

Holsti, K. J. (1871). Retreat from utopia: International relations theory, 1945-1970. *Canadian Journal of Political Science* 4, 2, June.

Huntford, Roland. (1972). *The New Totalitarians*. New York, New York: Stein and Day Publishers.

Inglehart, R. (1977). *The Silent Revolution*. Princeton, New Jersey: Princeton University Press.

International Herald Tribune. (1983). No, 3, 131, March 28:1.

International Labor Organization. (1985). *Apartheid in South Africa*. Geneva, Switzerland: ILO Publications.

Keohane, Robert O. and Joseph S. Nye. (1977). *Power and Interdependence*. Boston, Massachusetts: Little, Brown and Co.

Koblik, Steven. (1975). *Sweden's Development: From Poverty to Affluence, 1750-1970*. Minneapolis, Minnesota: University of Minnesota Press.

Korpi, W. (1979). Valfardsstatens variationer. *Sociologisk Forkning* xvi, 3:18.

Kunnie, Julian. (2000). *Is Apartheid Really Dead? Pan-Africanist Working-Class Cultural Critical Perspectives*. Boulder, Colorado: Westview Press.

Lambruch, G. (1977). Liberal corporation and party government. *Comparative Political Studies* 10:91-136.

Lewin, Leif et al. (1972). *The Swedish Electorate, 1887-1968*. Uppsala, Sweden: Almqvist and Wiksell Boktryckeri AB.

Lindbeck, Assar. (1974). *Swedish Economic Policy*. Berkeley, California: University of California Press.

Lindholm, Stig. (1971). *The Image of Developing Countries*. Uppsala, Sweden: Almqvist and Wicksell Boktrykeri AB.

LO/TCO. (1975). *South Africa: Black Labor, Swedish Capital*. Uppsala, Sweden: Offsetcenter AB.

Magnusson, Åke. (1974). *Swedish Investments in South Africa*. Uppsala, Sweden: The Scandinavian Institute of African Studies.

Mayer, Martin. (1983). *The Diplomats*. New York, New York: Doubleday and Co.

Mazrui, Ali M. (1977). *Africa's International Relations*. Boulder, Colorado: Westview Press.

McLaughlin, Martin M. (1979). *The United States and World Development Agenda, 1979*. New York, New York: Praeger Publishers.

Meidner, Rudolf. (1978). *Employees Investment Funds*. London, England: George Allen & Unwin.

Michanek, Ernest. (1971). *The World Development: A Swedish Perspective*. Stockholm, Sweden: Almqvist and Wiksell.

Millay, Norma. (1956 ed.). *Collected Poems of Edna St. Vincent Millay*. New York, New York: Harper and Row Publishers.

Miller, J. D. B. (1979). 'The Politics of International Aid.' In R. T. Shand and H. V. Richter, eds. *International Aid*. Canberra, Australia: The Australian National University.

Morgenthau, Hans. (1954). *Politics Among Nations*. New York: Alfred Knopf.

Mortimer, Robert A. (1984). *The Third World Coalition in International Politics*. Boulder, Colorado: Westview Press.

Myrdal, Gunnar. (1970). *The Challenge of World Poverty*. New York: Vintage Books.

National Central Bureau of Statistics. (1960-1985). *Statistical Abstract of Sweden*. Stockholm, Sweden: Norstedts Tryckeri.

Ndabazandie, Sabelo L. (09/26/1996). Killers for Apartheid. Available: http://www.lyastor.liu.se/nordic/murder/scsa960926.html

Nisbet, Robert A. (1969). *Social Change and History*. New York, New York: Oxford University Press.

Nogee, Joseph L. and Robert H. Donaldson. (1984). *Soviet Foreign Policy*. New York, New York: Pergamon Press.

Norberg, Viveca Halldin. (1977). *Swedes in Selassie's Ethiopia 1924-1952*. Uppsala, Sweden: Uppsala Offsetcenter AB.

OECD. (1980). *The OECD Report: Technical Change and Economic Policy*. Paris, France: OECD Publications.

Office for International Development Co-operation. (1978). *Guidelines for International Development Co-operation*. Stockholm, Sweden: OIDC.

O'Brien, Conor Cruise. (1962). *To Katanga and Back*. New York, New York: Simon and Schuster.

Organski, A. F. K. (1958). *World Politics*. New York: Alfred Knopf.

Owen, Roger and Bob Sutcliffe, eds. (1972). *Studies in the Theory of Imperialism*. Essex, Great Britain: Longman.

Pestoff, V. (1979). *Membership Participation in Swedish Consumer Cooperatives*. Stockholm, Sweden: Research Report.

Pestoff, V. (1977). *Voluntary Associations and Nordic Party Systems*. Stockholm, Sweden: Studies in Politics, No. 10.

Petterson, O. (1978). *Valjorna och Valet, 1976*. Stockholm, Sweden: Liber.

Pirages, Denis. (1978). *Global Ecopolitics*. Boston, Massachusetts: Duxbury Press.

Puchala, Donald J., ed. (1981). *Issues Before the 36th General Assembly of the United*

Nations, 1981-1982. United States: UN Association of the USA, Inc.

Reddy, E. S. (1989). *Olof Palme.* Available: http://www.anc.org.za/ancdocs/ history/ solidarity/palme-b.html

Regala, Roberto. (1959). *The Trends in Modern Diplomatic Practice.* Milano, Italy: Dott. A. Giuffre-Editore.

Resheter, John S., Jr. (1978). *The Soviet Polity.* New York, New York: Harper and Row Publishers.

Root, Franklin R. (1973). *International Trade and Investment.* Cincinnati, Ohio: South-Western Publishing Co.

Rose, R., ed. (1974). *Electoral Behavior.* New York: Free Press.

Rosenau, James N. (1971). Pre-theories and theories in foreign policy. In R. Barry Farrell, ed. *Approaches in Comparative International Politics.* Chicago, Illinois: Northwestern University Press.

Rostow, W. W. (1960). *The Stages of Economic Growth: A Non-Communist Manifesto.* Cambridge, Great Britain: Cambridge University Press.

Rudebeck, Lars. (1982). Nordic policies toward the Third World. In Bengt Sundelius, ed. *Foreign Policies of Northern Europe.* Boulder, Colorado: Westview Press.

Ruin, O. (1974). Participatory democracy and cooperation: The case of Sweden. *Scandinavian Political Studies* 9:171-184.

Russett, Bruce. (1976). *International Relations and the International System.* Chicago, Illinois: Rand McNally.

Sampson, Anthony. (1999). *Mandela: The Authorized Biography.* New York, New York: Alfred A. Knopf.

Santos, Theotonio Dos. (1970). The structure of dependence. *American Economic Review* lx, 2:231-236.

Scandinavian Institute of African Studies. (1977). *Nordic Statements on Apartheid.* Uppsala, Sweden: Offsetcenter AB.

Scandinavian Institute of African Studies. (1983-1986). Newsletters.

Scase, Richard. (1977). *Social Democracy in a Capitalist Society.* London, England: Croom Helm, Ltd.

Scott, Franklin D. (1975). *Scandinavia.* Cambridge, Massachusetts: Harvard University Press.

Schmitter, P. C. (1981). *Needs, Interests, Concerns, Actions, Associations, and Modes of Intermediation.* Berlin, Germany: IIM.

Schmitter, P. C. (1974). Still the century of corporatism. In F. B. Pike and T. Stritch, eds. *Corporatism: Socio-political Structures in the Iberia World.* Notre Dame, Indiana: University of Notre Dame Press.

Schnitzer, Martin. (1967). *The Swedish Investment Reserve.* Washington, DC: American Enterprise Institute.

Sellström, Tor. (1999). *Sweden and National Liberation in Southern Africa: Formation of a Popular Opinion (1950-1970).* Uppsala, Sweden: Nordiska Afrikainstitutet.

Sellström, Tor. (1999). *Sweden and National Liberation in Southern Africa: A Concerned Partnership (1970-1994).* Uppsala, Sweden: Nordiska Afrikainstitutet.

Sellström, Tor. (1999). *Liberation in Southern Africa—Regional and Swedish Voices:*

Interviews from Angola, Mozambique, Zimbabwe, Namibia, South Africa, the Frontline and Sweden. Uppsala, Sweden: Nordiska Afrikainstitutet.

SIDA. (1982). *Factablad: Sweden's Policy for International Developmen Co-operation Fiscal Year 1982/83.* Stcokholm, Sweden: SIDA Publications.

SIDA. (1982). *Sweden's Development Co-operation with Tanzania.* Stockholm, Sweden: SIDA Publications.

SIDA. (1982). *Factablad: Grants to Swedish Non-governmental Organizations' Development Assistance Projects.* Stockholm, Sweden: SIDA Publications.

SIDA. (1981). *Factablad: SIDA's Organization.* Stockholm, Sweden: SIDA Publications.

SIDA. (1980). *Factablad: Enlarged Co-operation.* Stockholm, Sweden: SIDA Publications.

SIDA. (1979). *Factablad: SIDA's Role in Decision Making on Development Co-operation with Individual Countries.* Stockholm, Sweden: SIDA Publications.

SIDA. (1978). *SIDA's Cooperation Program in Ethiopia.* Addis Ababa, Ethiopia: ETI-DCO Program Section.

SIDA. (1976). *Ethio-Swedish Development Co-operation.* Addis Ababa, Ethiopia: Royal Swedish Embassy.

Sigurdson, John and Ove Granstrand, eds. (1981). *Technological and Industrial Policy in China and Europe.* Lund, Sweden: Norstedts Trykerie.

Solvang, B. K. and J. Moren. (1974). Partsrepresentasjion i komitéer. *Den Kolegiale Forvaltning* 32-50.

Spero, Joan Edelman. (1985). *The Politics of International Economic Relations.* New York: St. Martin's Press.

Steinberg, S. H., ed. (1967-1982). *The Statesman's Yearbook.* New York: St. Martin's Press.

Steiner, Zara, ed. (1982). *The Times Survey of Foreign Ministries of the World.* London, England: Times Books, Ltd.

Stokke, Olav. (1978). *Svereges Utvecklingsbistånd och Biståndpolitik.* Uppsala, Sweden: Nordiska Afrikainstitutet.

Stokke, Olav and Carl Windstrand. (1973). *Southern Africa I and II.* Uppsala, Sweden: Nordiska Afrikainstitutet.

Sundelius, Bengt, ed. (1982). *Foreign Policies of Northern Europe.* Boulder, Colorado: Westview Press.

Swedish Institute. (1981, 1982). *Fact Sheets on Sweden, 1981, 1982.* Stockholm, Sweden: Swedish Institute Publications.

Swedish Institute of International Affairs. (1956). *Sweden and the United Nations.* New York: Manhattan Publishing Co.

Swedish Ministry of Economic Affairs. (1982). *Growth or Stagnation? The Swedish Economy, 1981-1985.* Stockholm, Sweden: MEA Publications.

Swedish Ministry of Finance. (1971). *The Swedish Economy, 1971-1975.* Stockholm, Sweden: Esselte Tryckeri.

Swedish Ministry of Foreign Affairs. (1978). *Documents on Swedish Foreign Policy 1975.* Stockholm, Sweden: Norstedts Tryckeri.

Swedish Secretariat for Futures Study. (1979). *Sweden in the New International Economic Order.* Stockholm, Sweden: Trosa Tryckeri AB.

Tomasson, Richard F. (1970). *Sweden: Prototype of Modern Society.* New York, New York: Random House.

Ul Haq, Mahbub. (1976). *The Poverty Curtain.* New York: Columbia University Press.

United Nations. (1981). *United Nations Today, 1981.* New York: UN Department of Public Information.

United Nations. (1962–1982). *Yearbook of International Trade Statistics.* New York: UN Publications.

UN Center Against Apartheid. (1978). *Solidarity with the Oppressed People of South Africa.* New York: United Nations Publications.

United States Congress. (1973). *US Diplomatic Relations with Sweden* (Hearings Before the House Committee on Foreign Affairs, 93rd Congress, 1st Session, September 12, 1973). Washington, DC: Government Printing Office.

Wadensjö, Gösta. (1979). *Meet Sweden.* Malmo, Sweden: Libertermods.

White, John. (1974). *The Politics of Foreign Aid.* New York: St. Martin's Press.

Wilber, Charles K., ed. (1979). *The Political Economy of Development and Underdevelopment.* New York: Random House.

Winstrand, Carl Gosta and Zdenek Čercenka. (1971). *Scandinavian Development Agreements with African Countries.* Uppsala, Sweden: Scandinavian Institute of African Studies.

Web Sites

http://216.109.117.135/search/cache?p=olof+palme+assassination+south+af
   rica&ei=UTF-8&url=J1Uvnmnbt(...9/23/03
http://archives.tcmie/irishexaminer/1999/06/02/fhead.htm
http://iafrica.com/news/sa/202557.htm
http://iafrica.com/news/sa/202863.htm
http://iafrica.com/news/sa/35028.htm
http://skog.de/enpalme1.htm
http://skog.de/enpalme2.htm
http://www.anc.org.za/anc/newsbrief/1996/news1022
http://www.sacc.org.za/news/Sweden.html
http://www.un.org/WCAR/statements/swedenE.htp
http://www.nnn.se/n-model/foreign/mandela.htm
http://www.num.org.za/News/misc/swedish.htm
http://www.karisable.com/palme.htm
http://www.suntimes.co.za/2003/01/26/news/news15.asp
http://www.wikipedia.org/wiki/Olof_Palme
http://www.student.sap.se/burma/aktuelt_konf_doc.htm
http://www.geocites.com/Athens/4795/SouthAfrica.htm
http://www.wprldlink.co.uk/stories/storyReader$434

http://www.567.co.za/news/world/27066.htm
http://www.idea.int/institute/Speeches/annalindh991216.html
http://www.iol.co.za/index.php?click_id=6&art_id=qw10632820180B223&
    set_id=1
http://news.bbc.co.uk/1/hi/world/europe/3098834.stm
http://news.bbc.co.uk/1/hi/world/europe/1262002.stm
wysiwg://61/http://www.guardian.co...uaries/story/0,3604,1040423,00.html
wysiwg://77/http://www.telegraph.c...tml?xml=/news/2003/09/12/db1201.xtml

Index

About the Author

Abdul Karim Bangura holds a Ph.D. in Political Science, a Ph.D. in Development Economics, a Ph.D. in Linguistics, and a Ph.D. in Computer Science. Bangura is currently a researcher-in-residence at the Center for Global Peace and a professor of International Relations in the School of International Service at American University. He is the United Nations Ambassador of the Association of Third World Studies (ATWS) and the director of The African Institution in Washington, DC. He is the author and/or editor of 36 other books and more than 270 scholarly articles. He is the Editor-in-Chief of both the *Journal of Research Methodology and African Studies* (JRMAS) and the *African Journal of Languages and Linguistics* (AJLL). He is the Immediate Past President of the Association of Third World Studies (ATWS) and a member of many other scholarly organizations. He has received numerous teaching and other scholarly and community service awards. He is also fluent in about a dozen African languages and six European languages, and is now learning Arabic and Hebrew.